WILLIAM SYDNOR

The REAL Prayer Book
1549 to the Present

MOREHOUSE-BARLOW CO., INC.
WILTON, CONNECTICUT

Acknowledgments

I thank the following publishers and other copyright owners for permission to quote from the works listed.

Macmillan, London and Basingstoke, for F. Proctor and W. H. Frere, *A New History of the Book of Common Prayer*, 1955, and G. J. Cuming, *A History of Anglican Liturgy*, 1969.

Oxford University Press, for P. Dearmer, *The Story of the Prayer Book*, 1933.

The Folger Shakespeare Library, for J. E. Booty, *The Book of Common Prayer—The Elizabethan Prayer Book*, 1976.

There are numerous quotations, principally from editorials and letters to the editor, which these periodicals have given me permission to use: *The Christian Challenge*, *The Churchman*, *The Living Church*, *The Witness*, and *Open—The Associated Parishes Newsletter*.

Historical Magazine of the Protestant Episcopal Church gave permission to quote from A. Dean Calcote, "The Proposed Prayer Book of 1785," Vol. XLVI, September, 1977.

Marion J. Hatchett gave permission to quote from "The Making of the First American Prayer Book," his doctor's dissertation, 1973.

If the author has inadvertently infringed any copyright, sincere apologies are offered.

Copyright © 1978 by William Sydnor
All rights reserved

Morehouse-Barlow Co., Inc.

ISBN 0–8192–1242–3
Library of Congress Catalog Card Number 78–61774

Printed in the United States of America

Preface

We Episcopalians love the Book of Common Prayer, but are often surprisingly uninformed about it. If we only knew more about this devotional treasury, we would love it even more! It is hoped that this book will help accomplish that end.

During the past decade Prayer Book revision has pushed worshippers into two categories—those who revel in it and those revolted by it. For the former it has been a time of insight, excitement, discovery, fulfillment, joy. For the latter it has been a time of baffling change, confusion, uncertainty, frustration, gloom—and strong, sometimes desperate, resistance. Those in both camps react the way they do for the same basic reason: they love the Prayer Book.

I feel certain that if Episcopalians knew the story of the long life of the Book of Common Prayer, their feelings about what is important and necessary and timeless might change. This would open doors of understanding between those two categories in which we now find ourselves, for a deeper awareness of our evolving devotional heritage may cause all of us to find anew that common ground of common prayer which is our legacy, our inspiration, and our joy.

So I am addressing this book to all those who love the Prayer Book.

If I succeed in being helpful, God be thanked and praised. I also thank the many who have assisted and encouraged me, these especially:

● My wife, Caroline, made the writing easier because she knows the demands, the discipline, the exasperations, and the satisfaction which come from trying to capture one's thoughts with a typewriter.

v

- The Rev. Marion J. Hatchett gave me advice, heartening support, and the invaluable use of his doctoral dissertation.
- The Rev. Leo Malania, Co-ordinator of Prayer Book Revision, has been most generous in opening his files to me.
- The Rev. Charles P. Price has helped more than he realizes with his shared insights from his wealth of liturgical knowledge.
- Dr. Ralph C. M. Flynt kindly put his extensive collection of Prayer Books and related materials at my disposal.
- The Rev. Reginald H. Fuller and Mrs. Joye Uzzell Pregnall both read the manuscript and made many valuable suggestions and gentle criticisms.

WILLIAM SYDNOR

February 21, 1978

Table of Contents

My advice is that you should make a careful selection of anything that you have found either in the Roman, or the Gallic, or any other Church, which may be more acceptable to Almighty God, and diligently teach the Church of the English. . . .

Choose, therefore, from each Church those things that are pious, religious, and seemly; and when you have, as it were, incorporated them, let the minds of the English be accustomed thereto.

    —Gregory the Great to Augustine of Canterbury, A.D. 601.[1]

I hope you will never hear from me any such phrase as our "excellent or incomparable Liturgy" . . . I do not think we are to praise the Liturgy, but to use it.

    —Frederick Denison Maurice, THE PRAYER-BOOK, Sermon I.[2]

CHAPTER I

Looking for the REAL Prayer Book

After the Proposed Prayer Book had been used in my congregation about six weeks, a regular worshipper asked, "Can't we use the *real* Prayer Book services part of the time?" His question raises a more profound one which comes into focus in terms of the Prayer Book experience of my family.

My father was baptized and confirmed using the Prayer Book of 1789. I was baptized and confirmed using the Prayer Book of 1892. My children were baptized and confirmed using the Prayer Book of 1928. Two years ago our granddaughter was confirmed in London using the Prayer Book of 1662. Which one of these is the *real* Prayer Book? And what of the other four Books? The two for which Thomas Cranmer, our liturgical "Father Abraham," was responsible in 1549 and 1552, the Elizabethan Book of 1559, and the 1604 Book on which James I put his mark?

Our Prayer Book is beautifully worded, spiritually uplifting, and biblically authoritative. However, as our world has changed, our lives have changed, our needs have changed, and our language has changed. Would the Prayer Book be so spiritually effective a guide if it had not changed in order to minister to each new day? Of course we bestow the name "the *real* Prayer Book" on the one we know the best. Is it for that reason only? Is there not a slightly uncomfortable feeling that perhaps one of the other versions about which we are ignorant might really be the treasure we assumed we had found? The way to lengthen the perspective of our appreciation is to examine the Prayer Book's venerable past. This will also enable us to stand taller in pride, stronger in conviction, and more reverent in our use of the *real* Prayer Book.

1

Let me be your guide on this trip through the more than 400 years of the Prayer Book's life. We will look at its long English-American story, the evolution from edition to edition, Thomas Cranmer's day to ours.

1549
1552
1559
1604
1662
1789
1892
1928
1976

We will explore the thickets and clearings of pressures and circumstances which led to the production of each one, see why each one was revised, look at the contents, and watch the reaction of our forefathers in the pews.

CHAPTER II

The First English Prayer Books—1549, 1552

The first Book of Common Prayer was published in March, 1549, and has come to be known as the First Book of Edward VI, the King of England at the time. It was not the work of one man, although Thomas Cranmer, Archbishop of Canterbury under Henry VIII and Edward VI, is certainly the mastermind behind it.

There were several conditions which interacted and resulted in the creation of that 1549 Book. The first of these was the fact that the Church of Cranmer's day functioned with at least six different liturgical books which had been in regular use in the West since the eleventh, possibly the ninth century—the *Missal* which contained the Canon of the Mass; the *Breviary* which contained the Daily Offices or Hour Services; the *Processional*, litanies which were used in procession; the *Manual* containing the occasional offices needed by a presbyter (baptism through burial); the *Pontifical*, rites conducted by a bishop; and the *Ordinal*, rules for the conduct of rites. These books were not universally the same; local usage dictated their contents. And there was widespread discontent with the medieval services.

There was also the renewal of scholarship in the Renaissance and a rediscovery of the Bible. These were the parents of an attitude of mind called "the New Learning." One indication of this New Learning which contributed toward subsequent liturgical reform was William Tyndale's translation of the New Testament in 1524.

In England two political events accelerated the momentum of liturgical reform. The first was that the attitude toward Lutheranism on the continent began to change, starting about 1532–34, the time when Henry VIII decided to break with Rome. The momentum of this changing attitude toward liturgical reform is reflected in the cascade of publications during the decade and a half between 1534 and the Act of Uniformity of 1549. Marion Hatchett lists 18 documents of various kinds which influenced the creation of that Prayer Book.[1]

During those same years the Bible was also caught up in the vortex of liturgical change. One of the ironies and also one of the indications of how fast events were moving is seen in what happened to Tyndale and his New Testament. When copies of his work which was printed in Cologne in 1525 reached England, Cardinal Wolsey and Henry VIII sent messengers to track him down and capture him, but he escaped to the continent where in 1535 he was arrested. In 1536 he was killed at the stake. Only one year after Tyndale had died for translating the New Testament into English, editions of the Sarum Primer appeared by order of Edward Lee, Archbishop of York, with the liturgical Epistles and Gospels in English. The translation was Tyndale's.

Epistles and Gospels in English were just a beginning. Within a year—1538—English Bibles were placed in every church by order of Cromwell, the King's Vicar-General. The order cautioned that they "might be read, only without noise, or disturbance of any public service, and without any disputation or exposition." In 1539 the Crown issued the Great Bible. It was the work of Miles Coverdale, who leaned heavily on the martyred Tyndale's translation. By 1543 the Convocation of Canterbury, the assembly of bishops and clergy,[2] had authorized the reading of "one chapter in English without exposition" after the *Te Deum* and *Magnificat*. This increasingly widespread substitution of English for Latin Scriptures opened the way for a similar change in the prayers.

So, as Percy Dearmer observes, the lectern from which the Bible is read reminds us of the first stage of reform which ultimately produced the Prayer Book.

The second political event which accelerated momentum toward liturgical reform occurred in 1544. Emperor Charles V of Spain sought the help of Henry VIII in forcing France to make peace. This gave new impetus to liturgical change in two ways. The first was that Henry ordered processions to be said or sung throughout the province of Canterbury—a normal practice in times of emergency. This occasioned the first Litany in

English, and it was full of phrases which later appeared in the Prayer Book. (So the Litany desk reminds us of the next stage of liturgical reform.) The second was that the determination of Catholic Charles V to subdue the Protestants on the continent caused a number of prominent continental divines to flee to England from persecution at home. Notable among these scholars were Peter Martyr (in December, 1547) and Martin Bucer (in April, 1549). Cranmer, the liturgical scholar, encouraged this influx of learned men. They arrived too late to influence the 1549 Book but they certainly contributed toward the revision in 1552.

Although all of these factors and pressures were moving the Church closer to significant liturgical change, nothing further happened during the closing years of Henry's reign. There was some experimentation with services in English but that was all.

Henry died in 1546; Edward VI came to the throne in January 1547. He was a boy of 11 years and was being brought up in the "New Learning." His religious inclinations were supported by the Protector, Somerset, and the rest of the Council. So experimentation with services in English began almost immediately. In the spring of 1549 Compline, Mattins, the Mass and Evensong were said in English in London, and the service on the anniversary of Henry VIII's death was sung in English at Westminster Abbey. These were probably early, perhaps experimental, drafts of the first Prayer Book Services.

The work of compiling the first Prayer Book got underway officially when Convocation appointed a committee consisting of Archbishop Cranmer and certain of "the most learned and discreet bishops, and other learned men" to "consider and ponder a uniform, quiet, and godly order." This committee of six bishops and six learned men met with the Archbishop at Chertsey Abbey on September 9, 1548. Four of them represented the "Old Learning," two were moderates, and the rest favored the "New Learning." Their discussions lasted only three weeks, "after which the New Order was delivered to the King at Windsor."

The committee was supposedly unanimously in favor of the proposed book, but in the debate in the House of Lords, it was evident that they were not, and when the final vote was taken Day, Skip, and Robertson, Bishops of Chichester, Hereford, and Westminster respectively, voted against it. Moreover, because the committee worked with such speed, they were no doubt working from a previously prepared draft. Cranmer had done a great deal of work on drafts of Mattins and Evensong which were already in print. The traditional Epistles and Gospels and the Litany were already in English. "The Order of Communion," which Parliament had authorized for use in March, 1548, needed little revision. Cranmer had been at work on the Services of Baptism and Matrimony. And various primers had Burial Services which pointed the way. The principal issue was the Canon of the Mass.

In December, 1548, the Houses of Parliament considered the first Prayer Book and on January 21, 1549, they passed the Act of Uniformity making it the official Prayer Book of the realm. The bishops in the House of Lords voted 10 to 8 for it. What action Convocation took is unknown. (The records of Convocation in this reign are incomplete.) On January 23 the King wrote to Bishop Bonner asserting that the Book was "set forth not only by the common agreement and full assent of the nobility and commons of the last session of the late Parliament but also by the like consent of the bishops in the same Parliament and of all other learned men of this realm in their synods and convocations provincial."[3] June 9, 1549, was the date fixed by the Act for the Book to be in use everywhere.

That first Book is described by Percy Dearmer as "an English simplification, condensation, and reform of the old Latin services, done with great care and reverence and in a genuine desire to remove the degeneracy of the Medieval rites by a return to antiquity."[4] It went on sale on Thursday, March 7, for 2 shillings in paperback, 3 shillings, 4 pence for hard cover. It was first used in "divers parishes in London" on the First Sunday in Lent, March 10. By Whitsunday (June 9) when it was to be in general use the price had risen to 2 shillings, 2 pence for paperback and 4 shillings for hard cover.

The book was entitled THE BOOKE OF THE COMMON PRAYER AND ADMINISTRATION OF THE SACRAMENTES, AND OTHER RITES AND CEREMONIES OF THE CHURCHE AFTER THE USE OF THE CHURCHE OF ENGLAND. That long title is saying that the book covers services previously contained in the Breviary, the Missal, the

Processional, and the Manual. The Pontifical section was added about a year later.

Were you to leaf through that Book here are some details which might catch your eye:

● Mattins (sometimes spelled Mattyns or Matins) and Evensong both begin with the Lord's Prayer and Versicles. The sequence of each service is the familiar one. The First Lesson is followed by the *Te Deum* or *Benedicite omnia opera* and the Second by the *Benedictus*. In Evensong the canticles are the *Magnificat* and *Nunc dimittis*. The Apostles' Creed is only indicated by a rubric. The Athanasian Creed is to be "sung or said" six times a year—Christmas, Epiphany, Easter, Ascension, Pentecost, and Trinity Sunday. There is no mention of the Creed in Evensong. Each service ends with the Third Collect. These two services simplify the devotions previously found in the Breviary. Mattins is a combining of medieval Mattins, Lauds, and Prime. Evensong combines Vespers and Compline. The "little hours" of Terce, Sext, and None are discarded. The pattern of two lessons is a break with the traditional three lessons.

● The title "The Supper of the Lorde and the Holy Communion, commonly called the Masse" suggests the sources. "The Supper of the Lorde" is the title Archbishop Hermann of Cologne (1536) used for the service. "The Masse" is both the medieval and Lutheran name for it. "The Holy Communion" is a vernacular name now for the first time applied to the whole service. The structure of the service is based closely on the medieval form. This is the order:

> The Lord's Prayer
> Collect for Purity—"Almighty God unto whom all hearts
>   are open...."
> Introit Psalm
> *Kyrie*
> *Gloria in excelsis*
> Collect of the day
> Prayers for the King
> Epistle
> Gospel
> Nicene Creed
> Sermon and/or an Exhortation

Offertory

Sursum Corda—"Lift up your hearts"

Sanctus

The Canon, beginning with the Prayer for the Whole State
    of Christ's Church and ending with the Lord's Prayer

The Peace—"The Peace of the Lord be always with you."

"Christ our Pascall lambe is offred for us. . . ."

The Invitation—"Ye who do truly and earnestly repent. . . ."

General Confession

Absolution

Comfortable Words

Prayer of Humble Access—"We do not presume to come. . . ."

Communion ("In the Communion tyme the Clarkes shall
    syng" the *Agnus Dei.*)

Postcommunion Thanksgiving

"The Peace of God. . . ."

The rubrics contain directives that those who intend to commune sit "in the quire, or in some convenient place nigh the
quire, the men on the one side, and the women on the other
side." They further direct that there be "Communion in both
kindes," that the wafers are to be "without all manner of print"
and be placed in the people's mouths, and that "all must attend
weekly, but need communicate but once a year." There is a
significant departure from the medieval Latin rite in the Prayer
of Consecration. The Latin rite had no invocation of the Holy
Spirit. The Latin rite accented the centrality of the Words of
Institution in the Middle Ages by such new ceremonies as the
Elevation of the Host. Cranmer corrected this straying from
tradition by inserting the invocation of the Holy Spirit from
Eastern practice (mainly the Eastern Liturgy of Saint Basil).
He inserted the words, "with thy Holy Spirit and Word vouchsafe to bless and sanctify these thy gifts of the bread and wine,"
before the Words of Institution. In that way he attempted to
bring together Eastern and Western ideas.

● The Litany is the same as the 1547 revision of Cranmer's
1544 Litany.

● The services here are those which in varying degrees were
based on the *Manual*—Baptism, Confirmation, Matrimony, Visitation of the Sick, Burial, Purification, and Commination (the Ash

Wednesday service). In Baptism the child is dipped "discretly
and warely" in the water three times. If, however, the child is
weak "it shall suffice to powre water upon it." The water is ordered to be changed once a month (Imagine the dusty scum and
sediment!) and new water blessed. The Catechism is included
along with the Confirmation Service. Here is the reason both for
its placement and for its contents: "All the Reformers laid great
stress on education, and particularly on religious education. . . .
Their Catechisms were not usually connected with Confirmation,
but were intended to cover the whole field of doctrine." Cranmer's
aim was different. He confined himself to the requirements of
godparents at the end of the Baptismal Service, namely, the
Creed, the Lord's Prayer, and the Ten Commandments. It was
the duty of godparents to teach their godchildren these formulas,
and by ancient tradition the children could not be confirmed
until they could repeat them.[5]

● At the end of the book are two appendices with self-explana-
tory titles—"Of Ceremonies" and "Certain Notes." The former
states that excess of ceremonies is wrong; meaningful ceremonies
are profitable; so "some be abolished and some retained." It
does not detail which ceremonies. "Certain Notes" states that
the minister shall wear a surplice for Mattins, Evensong, Baptism,
and Burial. But this is modified. The surplice is not an absolute
requirement save in colleges and cathedrals and for archdeacons,
deans, provosts, and the like. A country vicar is at liberty to
use a surplice or not. The Litany, Matrimony, Churching, and
Ash Wednesday are not mentioned, but as each of these is
normally followed by the Communion, it may be assumed that
th mass-vestments will be worn for them also. The bishop always
wears a rochet and carries his pastoral staff, unless it is held
by his chaplain; but no mitre is mentioned. The Communion
Service is conceived as essentially musical and the "clerks" who
lead the singing are directed to stay throughout the service
even if they are not intending to commune. (The musical setting
of John Merbecke, a minor canon of Windsor, came out in 1550.)
● The Ordinal was not a part of the 1549 Book. It was prepared the next year, published in March, 1551, and was annexed to the 1552 Book.

With Parliament's Act of Uniformity in January, 1549, and the actual use of the Book beginning in March of that year, the good ship Book of Common Prayer was launched on its stormy voyage and as of now has logged well over 400 years. During that time it has been overhauled and refitted for service eight times. For each of those eight times, as well as for the issuing of this first Book, the occasion has been one of joy or anguish, relief or disgust, pride or dismay, dedication or revolt. In 1549 such strong feelings as these poured over the Book almost before the ink was dry.

In producing the 1549 Book, Cranmer and his colleagues were sincerely and honestly seeking to lead the Church of England into a genuine revival of its worship practices. They aspired to help worshippers find greater meaning and significance in practices which were grounded in the rich heritage of Christendom. "Cranmer was trying to edge a nation notorious for its conservatism into accepting a reformed service, though, for all its comprehensiveness, the Book turned out to have gone almost too far. He hoped to satisfy the reforming zealots by suppressing all mention of oblation, to pacify the conservatives by keeping the time-hallowed framework, and to supply a positive, reformist-Catholic statement of what all had in common. This would provide the basis for further advance. For the moment, the more doctrinal positions that could be read out of it, the better." The attempt failed from every point of view. The conservatives disliked its innovations and the omission of old services; the reformers thought it retained too much of the old and did not go far enough in innovation.[6]

The law required that the Book be used everywhere beginning with Whitsunday, June 9, 1549. By Monday, ominous, open revolt against the government had erupted in many parts of England. While much of this was smoldering opposition to "the miserable government of the Protector and Council," some of it at least was due to worshippers' violent resentment of the new Prayer Book. Because of the danger of insurrection and the fear that France would find the widespread unrest an inviting opportunity to attack its old foe, the government was forced to secure its safety by foreign mercenaries.

The most violent of the revolts was in the West Country and was clearly a revolt by ordinary worshippers against the new changes in religion. They were adamant. "We demand the restoration of the Mass in Latin without any to communicate, and the Reservation of the Blessed Sacrament: Communion in one kind, and only at Easter: greater facilities for Baptism: the restoration of the old ceremonies—Holy-bread and Holy-water, Images, Palms, and Ashes. We will not receive the new service, because it is but like a Christmas game; but we will have our old service of Mattins, Mass, Evensong and processions in Latin, not in English."[7] They also demanded the recall of the English Bible "as tending to encourage heresy."

Parliament's Act of Uniformity had anticipated opposition to the Book, for it contained a penal statute regarding the enforcement of its use. Extreme measures by the government were therefore legally justified. By the end of August the uprising had been suppressed. Lord Russell and his foreign mercenaries stamped out all traces of it, distributed rewards, pardons, punishments, and, by the special direction of the Council, pulled down the bells out of the steeples in Devonshire and Cornwall, leaving only one, "the least of the ryng that now is in the same," to prevent their being used again in the cause of sedition. These were the elaborate steps the government had to take in order to enforce the adoption of the new Book.

All of that violent opposition was "due to the stiffest conservatism of men who did not wish even their least justifiable usage to be disturbed." This comment of Proctor and Frere is equally applicable to the reaction against almost every successive revision of the Book of Common Prayer. A characteristic of some Prayer Book worshippers seems to be that often their attachment to the services and ceremonies with which they are familiar is so great that they consider them the ultimate and final expression of Prayer Book worship, the end of liturgical history.

The less violent reactions to the 1549 Book ranged from one end of the ecclesiastical spectrum to the other. Princess Mary simply continued to have the old Mass said by her chaplains. Bishop Bonner took no steps to introduce the new book into the diocese of London until ordered to do so by the Council in August, after which he "did the office . . . sadly and discreetly." Indeed, the divided sympathies of the country were graphically mirrored in St. Paul's Cathedral, London. While Dean May was eagerly in favor of the reforms, Bishop Bonner was steadfast against them. Consequently, innovations were rapidly made, but old customs lingered on much longer than the reformers liked. Bishop Bonner persisted in his opposition and was finally publicly denounced, imprisoned, and on October 1 deprived of his see.

The conservatives grasped at any pretext to avoid change. "The fall of the Protector, Somerset, in the autumn of 1549 gave rise to the rumor that the Book would be withdrawn, and some of the Oxford colleges actually reintroduced the Mass. The Council, now led by Warwick, reacted vigorously, and issued an Order calling in all copies of the medieval service-books (with the exception of the pontificals, which had not yet been superseded), to be defaced and abolished."[8]

In the forefront of church leaders who were pushing for even greater reform were Bishops Hooper and Ridley. John Hooper, a leading English disciple of Zwingli, the continental reformer, pronounced the book "defective, and of doubtful construction, and, in some respects indeed, manifestly impious." He was thrown into prison for refusing to wear the proper vestments at his own service of consecration as Bishop of Gloucester. Eventually he "agreed to wear the vestments for the occasion, so long as he was not expected to wear them in his diocese." Ridley, transferred to London in April, 1550, led a drive against those practices which remotely suggested perpetuation of the Mass, such as the priest's kissing the Lord's Table, washing his fingers, ringing of sacring bells. He urged incumbents and churchwardens to replace their high altar with a table set in the place "thought most meet by their discretion and agreement." This was done in St. Paul's in June. The table was placed in a diversity of positions. Bishop Ridley had it standing east and west "in the midst of the upper quire," with the minister on the south side. At the same time he had the iron grates of the quire bricked up, to prevent anyone from watching the communion without communicating.

The 1549 Book expressly referred to "the Altar," never a holy table. Ridley along with Hooper was a prime mover in the widespread destruction of "the altars of Baal." This was both high-handed and illegal. Rich hangings, jewels, gold and silver plate were removed and destroyed, or simply disappeared. Some courtiers desired their destruction because they hoped to enrich themselves. So there was plunder of valuable furniture, and in its stead "an honest table." Throughout the country, church walls were being limewashed and the Royal Arms and Scripture texts replaced medieval wall paintings. By the end of young King Edward's reign there had been a clean sweep of all that was worth stealing: the churches, their chests, their treasures had been ransacked. It was a tragic time. The Edwardian robbers were not genuine reformers, but they certainly helped destroy the manner of worship which had gone on under the 1549 Prayer Book by their looting of the ornaments. The work of destruction which they began was to be continued by the Puritans in the next century. In an attempt to reconcile parishioners to the loss of their ornaments and altars, the Council stepped in after the fact with an order to bishops on November 4, 1550, to remove altars and replace them with holy tables.

The campaign to bring about reform was reflected in the evolving leadership of the Church. Older bishops were gradually replaced by men of the New Learning. Gardiner and Bonner were sent to prison for preaching against the new doctrine of the Eucharist; Heath was deprived of his see for refusing to accept the Ordination Service, Day for refusing to remove altars, and Rugg resigned.

The influence of the New Learning had begun to reach England by the early 1530s. Cranmer had first experienced Lutheran worship in Lent, 1532, at Nuremberg. He was no doubt familiar with Martin Bucer's book (1524) on "the Lord's Supper." This was a new name for the ancient sacrament, a name which found its way into the 1549 Book. Bucer was "the leading light of the religious life" of the city of Strasbourg, Germany. It is not surprising that when life on the continent became intolerable for protestant reformers, Cranmer invited Bucer to come to England. This he did in April, 1549. By the end of the year Bucer, whose views on the sacrament were somewhere between those of Calvin and those of Zwingli, had the Divinity Chair at Cambridge. Peter Martyr was another reformer who crossed the Channel. He was an Italian whom the Inquisition drove out of Italy. Zurich and Strasbourg were only temporary havens for him before coming to England. In less than a year he was appointed Regius Professor of Divinity at Oxford. He and Bucer were friendly rivals. These two were in the forefront of the continental reformers who put their mark on the Second Prayer Book of Edward VI.

Continental pressure for reform reached England by mail packet as well as in person. Calvin, "the Geneva Pope," was graciously pleased to say that the Book contained "many tolerable absurdities." He called for more drastic changes. Actually the first Book was too conservative for all of the continental reformers. While they were thankful for it, they obviously hoped for and expected further revision. They considered the retention of ceremonies as only a temporary expedient.

It is not surprising that because of English extremists such as Hooper and Ridley and continental reformers like Bucer and Peter Martyr, the pressure for revising the 1549 Book began almost from the moment of publication. By August, 1549, the translation of the *Te Deum* had been improved, and the Litany had been placed between Evensong and the Sacrament. (Its 1549 position had been right after the Lord's Supper.)

One unintentional cause for the extremely reformist nature of the revision came out of the trial of Bishop Gardiner. He was being tried for preaching against the doctrine of the Eucharist. In his defense he presented a paper, "An Explication and Assertion of the true Catholic Faith," which was a reply to Cranmer's "Defence of the True and Catholic Doctrine of the Sacrament of the Body and Blood of our Saviour Christ." Gardiner's method was both clever and exasperating. He picked out various passages in the 1549 Book which appeared to express the Catholic doctrine rather than Cranmer's, and warmly commended them. The only way to stem this kind of opposition was to alter the text at these points. So the effect of Gardiner's criticisms was to make the next revision more narrowly Reformed in doctrine, and harder for well-disposed Catholics to accept.

No conclusive consideration of the proposed revision took place in the Houses of Convocation. The moderates had been repressed, and their leaders—Bishops Gardiner, Bonner, Heath, Day, Tunstal, and perhaps others—were in the Tower. In Parliament the Second Act of Uniformity was considered for a month and passed on April 14, 1552. The Book was to become official on November 1 of that year.

Perhaps for appearances' sake that Second Act of Uniformity spoke favorably of the 1549 Book. It was "a very godly order, agreeable to the Word of God and the primitive Church, very comfortable to all good people." Percy Dearmer observed that "the First Prayer Book was indeed too fair-minded for the violent and bitter spirit of the age."

The Act justifies the revision as having two purposes: "more plain and manifest explication," and "more perfection of . . . some places where it is necessary . . . to stir Christian people to the true honoring of Almighty God." In a sort of halfhearted way these purposes were followed. For example, in relation to the former, "The Purification of Women" is changed to "The Thanksgiving of Women After Childbirth, commonly called the Churching of Women." The latter may be identified with "the requirement of saying the Office daily . . . more congregational participation, especially in the Creeds and the Lord's Prayer (though not, as Bucer suggested, in the Prayer of Humble Access and Thanksgiving); communion at least three times a year, instead of once . . . and above all, a new introduction to both Holy Communion, and Mattins and Evensong. In pursuance of a general policy of dropping the old names, the latter are now called Morning and Evening Prayer, while 'the Mass,' 'anthems,' and 'Ash-Wednesday' no longer appear anywhere in the book. . . . Morning and Evening Prayer are to be said where 'the people may best hear,' not necessarily in the quire; but the chancels are to 'remain as they have done,' not be shut up, as Hooper wished."[9]

In the interval between the closing of Parliament (April 14, 1552) and the beginning of use set by the Second Act of Uniformity (November 1, 1552), a great controversy arose over kneeling to receive communion. The reformers were dead set against the practice and John Knox, who had become the Royal Chaplain, was as outspokenly opposed in London as he had been in the north. The Council awoke to the fact that the Book, now already in print (September 27), specifically required kneeling. The Council held up the Book on the pretext of a printer's error and wrote Cranmer to reconsider. He refused to take any action and at the same time pointed out "both the crudity of the Scriptural argument which was being alleged against the custom, and also the indecency of sitting to receive, but kneeling both before and after reception." On October 27, four days before the Book was to go into use, a letter went forth from the Council to the Lord Chancellor "to cause to be joined unto the Book of Common Prayer lately set forth a certain declaration, signed by the King's Majesty and sent unto his Lordship, touching the kneeling at the receiving of the Communion." So the Council compromised the matter on the eve of publication with the Black Rubric, which declared in explanation of the requirement to kneel to receive "that it is not ment thereby, that any adoration is doone, or oughte to bee doone, either unto the Sacramental bread or wyne, there bodily receyued, or unto anye reall or essencial presence there beeyng of Christ's naturall fleshe and bloude."

Procter and Frere conclude, "Thus against the Archbishop's will and without the consent of the Church, English religion reached its low water mark and the ill-starred Book of 1552 began its brief career."[10]

Take a brief look at the principal changes in this Second Book.

●Morning and Evening Prayer now have a penitential introduction—Opening Sentences, Invitation, Confession, and Absolution. This introduction was added because, on those many occasions when there was no Communion (the service would end with the Offertory), there would be no expression of penitence and forgiveness. By adding this at the beginning of Morning Prayer, the need was met.

● The Litany now follows Evening Prayer and has this more elaborate title: "Here followeth the Letany to be used upon Sundayes, Wednesdayes, and Fridayes, and at other times, when it shall be commanded by the Ordinary." Several new occasional prayers have been attached to it—for rain, for fair weather, in the time of dearth and famine, in the time of war, and in the time of any common plague or sickness. The last of these was added because of the "sweating sickness" which swept the country in the summer of 1551.

● Percy Dearmer says, in the Holy Communion, "Cranmer set forth his matured conclusions."[11] The Decalogue has been added. (There is no Summary of the Law in either of these first Books.) The Prayer for the Whole State of Christ's Church has been separated from the Canon and follows the Offertory. Significantly, the introduction to that prayer now reads "Let us pray for the whole state of Christes Church militant here in earth." All references to the saints and the departed are removed. The order of the major part of the service is that which is more familiar to present-day users of the Prayer Book than to users of the First Book:

> Invitation
> General Confession
> Absolution
> Comfortable Words
> *Sursum Corda*
> *Sanctus*
> We do not presume ...
> Prayer of Consecration
> Reception
> Lord's Prayer
> Oblation or Thanksgiving
> *Gloria in excelsis*
> The Peace of God

The Invitation ("Ye who do truly and earnestly repent ..."), Confession, Absolution, and Comfortable Words now come before the *Sursum Corda*. The Prayer of Consecration does not follow the same order as that in the first Book. Cranmer considered the different form to be more in accord with the New Testament. There is a whole series of changes aimed at removing any suspicion of transubstantiation. For instance, instead of praying that the bread and wine "may be unto us the body and blood," the prayer now asks that we "may be partakers of the body and blood." There is also strong emphasis on the memorial nature of the sacrament. This is most notably present in the Words of Administration. The traditional words which became part of the 1549 Book are "The body of our Lord Jesus Christ which was given for thee, preserve thy body and soul unto everlasting life." In 1552 those words were dropped and in their place: "Take and eat this, in remembrance that Christ died for thee, and feed on him in thy heart by faith, with thanksgiving." The rubric states that the people receive in both kinds "in their handes kneling." Also because of suspicion of tran-

substantiation the *Benedictus* ("Blessed is he that cometh...")
and the *Agnus Dei* are omitted. And of course there is the Black
Rubric referred to earlier (page 16) which states emphatically
that by kneeling to receive "it is not meant thereby that any
adoration is done or ought to be done either unto the Sacramental bread or wine. . . ." The doctrinal impact of the sacrament
centers in what it says about the presence of Christ in the
Eucharist. The 1549 Book was consistent with the Catholic
belief in the real presence. But, as Procter and Frere observe,
the 1552 Book makes it clear that the Prayer of Consecration
refers rather to the worshippers than to the elements, and that
the presence of Christ is not in the Sacrament but only in the
heart of the believer. So the Book is more acceptable to those
"determined to retain the primitive doctrine apart from mediaeval
accretions." The final change in the service was to remove the
Gloria in excelsis from its ancient position following the *Kyrie*
and place it just before the Benediction. It thus becomes a new
climax at the end of the service.

● The Baptismal Service is vigorously remodeled. The entire
service is to take place at the font. Bucer suggested that it take
place in the context of the Communion Service. On this point
he was 400 years ahead of his time! The sign of the cross is
kept in spite of the objections of the reformers. The latter part
of the Service established the pattern followed in all succeeding
Books up through 1928. The exorcism, the anointing, the putting
on of the Chrysom, and the triple repetition of immersion are
all omitted. And the rubric which gives sanitary-minded moderns
a sigh of relief directs that the font be filled and the water
consecrated whenever the service is used rather than only once
a month.

● The Burial Office is curtailed. There are no prayers for the
dead and a special office for Eucharist at funerals is omitted. The
minister is not directed to throw dust into the grave.

The Book is very careful to omit any mention of "the Altar."
It simply refers to "the Table" or in one place to "Goddes
borde." The manual acts which might suggest transubstantiation

are eliminated—the fraction and elevation of the hosts. Ordinary bread is used and is put in the communicants' hands.

The only vestments permitted are a rochet for bishops and a surplice for priests and deacons. Even a hood or a scarf is forbidden.

Music is virtually abolished in Holy Communion except the *Gloria in excelsis* which is permitted to be sung as an alternative to saying it. Introit Psalms, *Kyrie,* Creed and *Sanctus* are all said. Two months before the Book came out, the organ at St. Paul's, London, ceased to be used.

A rubric directs that the Table stand in the body of the church or in the chancel (the place for best audibility), and that it be covered with a fair linen cloth. The priest is to stand at the north side.

The wardens collect the alms rather than the people coming up with them.

The Zwinglian reformers pressed hard for the utmost simplicity of dress, furnishing, and movement. Certainly their influence can be seen throughout the Book, but evidence of other doctrines is also there. Percy Dearmer gives this often-unappreciated 1552 Book significant credentials: "Proud as we are of the First Model [1549 Book], there is no less cause for pride in the Second, when we remember that its purpose is to provide a liturgy that is Apostolic rather than Patristic."[12]

This Second Book of Edward VI, which became official on November 1, 1552, was unpopular everywhere. It was half-heartedly launched on its brief career—no authorization was even given for its use in Ireland. Conservative priests made the best of it for the moment by retaining old ceremonial. There was little or no violence. Opposition to the use of upsetting practices had spent itself during the two years or more prior to the appearance of the Book.

Young King Edward died July 5, 1553, and Mary, the ardently Roman Catholic daughter of Henry VIII and Catherine of Aragon, came to the throne. With the news of Edward's death, the Latin Mass was immediately and widely restored. The 1552 Book was only officially in use for eight months.

CHAPTER III

The Book of 1559

Elizabeth became queen November 17, 1558, and a new day dawned in the religious life of England. The Protestant exiles returned from the continent full of extreme reaction to the unbending Romanism of Mary's reign. What form of worship would now become the official one?

Elizabeth assured the Spanish ambassador that her purpose was to restore religion to the form it had had under her father, Henry VIII. But this was nearly impossible. There was no longer an appreciable base of support for such a stance. Some of the former proponents were dead, some had been converted. Moreover, the returned exiles made further steps toward Protestantism inevitable.

The religious direction in which England would move depended on the Queen and the religious leaders whom she appointed and whom she supported. What was she like? What were her private religious and philosophical views? John Booty gives us this description:

She was a Protestant-humanist who read Socrates and Cicero, Saint Cyprian and Philip Melanchthon, and who was well acquainted with the works of Desiderius Erasmus. Ascham said in 1570 that the Queen "readeth here now at Windsor more Greek every day than some prebendary of this church doth read Latin in a whole week." Indeed, she was accustomed to reading some part of Erasmus' Greek New Testament daily. Her religion was not that of the zealous—she could not approve of John Knox and his ways. It was that of the Christian humanist, involving devotion and moderation, and delighting in beauty, the beauty of a perfect literary style, the beauty of orderly religious ceremony. It was a religion linked to national sentiment, with the conviction that God was doing a mighty thing, through his Deborah, for England and, through England, for the world.[1]

20

So the Queen sided with "the small but sensible moderate party." Very shortly this resulted in the authorization of the 1552 Book relieved of its more extreme features. But in the meantime firm action had to be taken to avoid religious chaos. To end disorders resulting from violent sermons on both sides, a royal proclamation was issued on December 27, 1558, forbidding all preaching. The Epistle, Gospel, and Ten Commandments were to be read in English as was being done in the Queen's chapel "until consultation may be had by Parliament." But there were ceremonial tensions, even in the Queen's chapel. On Christmas Day (Elizabeth had been on the throne five weeks) when Bishop Oglethorpe was saying Mass in the Royal Chapel, she sent a message to him during the singing of the *Gloria*, ordering him not to elevate the host, because she did not like the ceremony. The Bishop refused, and the Queen left after the Gospel.

It was going to be a delicate matter to revise and adopt an acceptable Prayer Book, and it seems that the Queen followed the cautious warning of Armagil Waad that the matter would require "great cunning and circumspection."

And no doubt the Queen did intend to proceed cautiously. Her plan was to follow the Edwardian pattern by permitting communion in both kinds, then after leisurely consultation to have a new Act of Uniformity passed, perhaps in the autumn, with a Prayer Book attached. Perhaps that would have been the ideal way to proceed; however, conditions dictated otherwise. On the one hand, the exiles were impatient and pressing. Elizabeth realized that if she did not accept the 1552 Book she might be faced with a demand for the Genevan *Form of Prayers*. On the other, because peace had been signed with France, there was now no need to attach much weight to the wishes of papal Catholics. So the 1552 Book was adopted with a few revisions—changes in the direction of the 1549 Book. The Queen and her government showed that they were independent of the more zealous Protestants by rejecting any revisions that would make the Book more Protestant and by adopting revisions that could only be interpreted as conservative. This religious settlement was to Elizabeth what was possible and best for the nation and she would not countenance any major adjustment of it. If there could be no revival of 1549, there would certainly be no movement in Calvin's direction.

The Act of Uniformity was passed in April, 1559. Convocation was not even consulted, and it passed by only three votes; in the House of Lords nine bishops voted against it. Percy Dearmer concludes that "The consent of the Church can thus only be claimed by virtue of its subsequent acquiescence."[2] It became the official Book on the Feast of the Nativity of St. John the Baptist, June 24, 1559, and the penalties for failure to use it were severe—a fine of one year's stipend and six months imprisonment for the first offense, forfeit of all "spiritual promotions" and one year imprisonment for the second, life imprisonment for the third.

These are the significant changes in the 1559 Book as compared with the 1552 Book:

● Morning and Evening Prayer were read in the choir "with a loud voice" rather than, as 1552 put it, "in such place . . . as the people may best hear." The other rubric at the beginning of Morning Prayer, known as "The Ornaments Rubric," states that "the minister at the time of the Communion, and at all other times in his ministration, shall use such ornaments in the church as were in use by authority of Parliament in the second year of the reign of King Edward the Sixth." This has cast long shadows of influence across the Church for centuries. The second year of Edward VI was 1548. So, on the question of vestments and ornaments the Elizabethan Book disallows the puritanical bareness of ornament which characterized the 1552 Book. In every other respect Morning and Evening Prayer are identical with the previous Book. They both end with the Third Collect.

● The Litany was the only service in English used during Mary's reign. Of course, when it was used that offensive petition in the 1552 Book which prayed for deliverance "from the tyranny of the Bishop of Rome, and all his detestable enormities" was dropped. Now this edited version of the Litany appears in the Elizabethan Book. A similar reference to the Pope's "usurped power and authority" has also been dropped from the ordination services. These polemic phrases were unnecessary and likely to be embarrassing to those conducting diplomatic affairs among

Continental Catholics. A prayer for the Queen has been added
at the end of the Litany and also, following "A Prayer of
Chrysostom," there appears for the first time II Corinthians
13:14, which in time came to be known as "The Grace."

● The rubric at the beginning of Holy Communion reads: "The
Table having at the Communion time a fair white linen cloth
upon it, shall stand in the body of the church, or in the chancel,
where Morning and Evening Prayer be appointed to be said.
And the priest standing at the north side of the Table shall
say..." The sequence and content of the service are those of
the 1552 Book with two exceptions. The Words of Administration combine those of 1549 and 1552. 1549: "The body of our
Lord Jesus Christ which was given for thee, preserve thy body
and soul into everlasting life"; and 1552: "Take and eat this, in
remembrance that Christ died for thee, and feed on him in
thy heart by faith, with thanksgiving." The Black Rubric of
1552 regarding the meaning of kneeling to receive communion
is dropped.

To the great displeasure of the Genevan party, church music
was officially encouraged. The *Injunctions* of 1559 included this
directive for parish churches: "For the comforting of such that
delight in music, it may be permitted that in the beginning or
in the end of the common prayers, either at morning or at
evening, there may be sung an hymn or such-like song to the
praise of Almighty God, in the best sort of melody and music
that may be conveniently devised, having respect that the sen-
tence of him may be understanded and perceived."[3]

John Day published a book of services for four voices in
1565; in several of them the whole of the congregation's part
is set to music. This was also true of Thomas Tallis' "Dorian."
It soon became the custom to set only the *Kyrie* and the Creed
to music. This may have been because the practice of ending
the morning service with Ante-Communion on three Sundays
out of four was becoming general. However, the normal Sunday
service was thought of as Morning Prayer, Litany, and Holy
Communion.

In collegiate chapels and some parish churches there were
bequests for the maintenance of a choir. Plainsong was generally
used for the canticles and the Psalms. Sometimes on great

festivals harmonized settings were used. The *Injunctions* of 1559 made it permissible to sing compositions with English texts; often they were parts of the Collect, Epistle, or Gospel of the day. These acquired the name of "anthem"—a variant of "antiphon." The organist was permitted to play an organ solo during the offertory at Communion, and short voluntaries were sometimes inserted between the lessons and canticles.

In the age of Elizabeth edification was the primary aim in worship. Two characteristics of that worship makes this evident. First, this emphasis is reflected in the attitude toward the aesthetic. While church music was certainly not ignored during the Elizabethan period, the Church sought to subject it and everything else to the principle of edification. The Creed, the Lord's Prayer, and the Ten Commandments were set in large letters on the east wall. So it was the basis of Christian faith in words that took the place of images and pictures. Religion was becoming more and more word-centered and intellectual— a matter of reason and reasonableness. Secondly, the tone of worship itself pointed in the direction of edification. It was solemn, impressive, and penitential. Morning Prayer, the Litany, and Ante-Communion were the didactic and penitential preparation for the occasional Holy Communion and for the living of the Christian life.

● The Occasional Offices, Baptism through Burial, remained just as they were in the 1552 Book. The only change in the Ordinal was the deletion of derogatory references to the Pope as noted above. The Queen's sovereignty over the Church within her realm was clearly stated as "against the power and authority of any foreign potentates."

● In May 1552 the Privy Council issued Forty-two Articles endeavoring to enforce some of the doctrines of the Continental Reformers upon the English Church. The Church was not invited to sanction these articles but the Council had the effrontery to state on the title-page that they had been agreed upon by the bishops in Convocation. In 1562 the Forty-two Articles were reduced to Thirty-nine. Article 42, which had asserted the existence of Hell in terms very moderate for the times, disappeared forever.

The reinstituting of Prayer Book order met with little opposition. While there were places where devout congregations continued to flock to the Latin Mass, almost as soon as Elizabeth became Queen there were many places where the people "entirely renounced the Mass" and by early January were bringing back the Prayer Book. On Easter, several weeks before the actual Act of Uniformity had passed, the service in the Royal Chapel was Mass "sung in English according to the use of King Edward," and after it the celebrant took off his vestments and gave Communion in both kinds to the Queen and many peers, vested only in a surplice. By Whitsunday (May 14) a number of parish churches and the monks at Westminster made haste to follow suit. St. Paul's was the only church in London which retained the Latin services up until the last minute.

The actual transition was very quietly accomplished. The resistance of the bishops and principal clergy was both strenuous and solid, but this does not seem to have been the case among the rank and file; most suffered in silence, though certainly many of them deprecated change. In the changeover from the Roman Catholic days of Mary to Elizabeth's Protestant regime, not more than some 200 clergy were deprived of their livings during the years 1558–1564, a state of things which is in marked contrast with the wholesale policy of deprivation by which the Marian ecclesiastical policy was carried through.

During the 45 years Elizabeth was on the throne the Prayer Book was under attack by the Puritans on the left and the Roman Catholics on the right. The Prayer Book was only a part of that religious struggle out of which was forged the genius of what has come to be called "Anglicanism." And it is that part—the fortunes of the Prayer Book in Elizabethan England—which we now seek to appreciate.

The most persistent and uncompromising attacks on the Prayer Book came from the Puritans. With the Act of Uniformity, the Prayer Book party in Parliament won the day. But the exiles who had come streaming back to England after the death of Queen Mary had hoped to have the 1552 Book as revised and used in Frankfurt. What they got was 1552 revised in the other direction. Their annoyance must have been great when the revision swept away several of the Puritan portions of Edward's Second Book and brought back some of the discarded ceremonies and vestments of earlier times. They were disillusioned by the Queen's conservatism, but this did not keep them from trying by various means to further reform in Convocation, in Parliament, and, if need be, independently. Their two main principles were that nothing is admissible that is not actually found in Scripture; and that nothing tainted with Romanism is admissible, even if it is mentioned in Scripture. Strict observance of these principles ruled out the use of the surplice, wafer bread, the sign of the cross in baptism, kneeling for communion, the ring in marriage, the veil in churching, bowing at the name of Jesus, and the use of organs and "effeminate and over-refined" music. In Baptism it was in their minds an usurpation of the father's responsibility that the minister should address the infant and the godparents answer in its name. Other reprehensible practices included emergency baptism by women, Confirmation, the preaching of sermons at funerals, and, unexpectedly, the reading of the Bible in church. In the first decade there was little criticism of the Prayer Book text beyond what was involved in these practices.

The Puritans believed that the vision of God was obscured by decorative display. Of course an excess of ornament is a real danger if simplicity and sincerity are forgotten, but Puritan excesses were "the insanity of a wild reaction, a kind of Romanism turned inside out."[4] Altars were destroyed in a riotous and unauthorized fashion. This was brought in check by a royal injunction which declared

that no altar be taken down but by the oversight of the curate of the church and the churchwardens . . . and that the holy table in every church be decently made and set in the place where the altar stood, and at Communion time should be so placed within the chancel that the minister be conveniently heard, and the communicants conveniently communicated.[5]

As early as 1562 a determined attempt was made in Convocation to abolish the ceremonies (and also the organ) against which Puritan opposition was to wage such a lengthy contest. The proposal lost in the lower house of Convocation by only one vote, even in spite of the Queen's opposition! And it was her decisive action alone which prevented the House of Commons from perpetrating that wholesale vandalism.

A decade later, in 1571, a bill was brought into Parliament "for Reformation of the Book of Common Prayer," mainly aimed at the disputed ceremonies. The House was warned that ceremonial matters were reserved to the Queen's authority, and in a few days Strickland (who had presented the measure in Parliament) was called before the Council for infringing upon the Royal prerogative. It was only after some days and after some protests from the House that he was allowed to resume his place in it. The Queen was in the thick of the fight.

This evident Royal displeasure did not prevent another similar attempt the following year. A bill of Rites and Ceremonies was read three times in the Commons and referred to a committee; "but two days later a Royal message ordered 'that from henceforth no bills concerning religion shall be preferred or received into this house unless the same shall first be considered and liked by the clergy.' The agitation against the Prayer Book was at this time going on all over the country, and six months later drew from the Queen 'A proclamation against the despisers and breakers of the orders prescribed in the Book of Common Prayer.' "[6]

A fundamental reason for the general Puritan reaction against the Prayer Book outside of Parliament was not political leadership but personal piety. This came about because of the Genevan Bible which was published in 1560. (The slang name for it is "the Breeches Bible" because of the translation of Genesis 3:7— "The eyes of them bothe were opened, and they sewed figge-tree leaves together, and made themselves breeches.") It was printed in modern type and was the popular version of the English people. It was full of Calvinistic notes, and a Calvinistic Catechism was bound up with it. Hence the book spread Calvinistic doctrine everywhere..

The final Puritan attack on the Prayer Book during Elizabeth's reign came in the 1580s. In both 1586 and 1587 proposals were made in Commons to substitute *A Book of the Form of Common Prayers,* a Genevan book, for the Book of Common Prayer. On the second occasion, three days after the House adjourned, Mr. Cope, who presented the proposal, and three of his supporters were sent to the Tower by the Council. The Queen sent for both sets of proposals and suppressed them. However, that book was already being secretly used in some quarters.

After these failures Puritan opposition became more secret
in its methods. The disloyalty to the Prayer Book, both as to
services and ceremonies, continued. Emasculated editions of
the Prayer Book appeared and were illegally used in secret.
However, nothing formal was done until after Elizabeth's reign.

Now look at opposition from the Roman Catholics. Recusants
and separatists on the conservative side objected to any reform
and clung to Roman obedience. Here also the Prayer Book
was the battleground. In the early days of the reign there was
good reason for believing that Pope Pius IV was prepared to
recognize the Prayer Book in return for a recognition of his
own supremacy. The conflict, however, became more and more
bitter, and the Roman authorities forbade attendance at the
English Services (October 2, 1562). Finally, when Pope Pius V
published his Bull of excommunication (1570), all prospect
of reconciliation on that side was shut from view. In 1588 the
defeat of the Spanish Armada removed any serious danger
from the papists. It was then that the Queen felt free to take
a stronger line with the Puritans.

The Elizabethan compromise, on a middle ground between
the fanatical Puritans and the embittered Romans—known as
the Elizabethan settlement—was never fairly accepted. The 1559
Book was used in mutilated form. No one carried out in full
the ceremonial directions. Because the Ornaments Rubric was
ignored, the "Advertisements" issued in 1566 were an attempt
to secure at least a minimum of conformity—the surplice, hood,
and cope, with frontal and fair linen for the holy Table. Of
course, there was strong official support all along for the use
of the organ, the cross in baptism, kneeling for communion, and
the wedding ring, all of which nettled the Puritans.

While there was no official revision of the 1559 Book, there
was modification in practice. Injunctions issued in 1571 by
Edmund Grindal, Archbishop of York, ordered: "All parishioners
are to receive the Communion three times a year besides Ash
Wednesday, namely, on one of the two Sundays before Easter,
Pentecost, and Christmas; the Epistle and Gospel are to be
read in the pulpit or stall; and the minister is to make no pause
between Morning Prayer, the Litany, and the Holy Communion,
so that nobody should go out without attending 'the whole
divine service.'"[7]

In 1594 Richard Hooker's monumental work, *Laws of Ecclesiastical Polity*, began to appear. Volume V (1597) dealt with the Prayer Book. He was writing at leisure and not in the heat of religious dissension or political upheaval. Moreover, he had "an enormous armoury of patristic learning, reinforced by effective appeals to pastoral experience." This studied treatment of the Prayer Book provided its *raison d'être*, and became the bulwark of its understanding, appreciation, and defense for generations of churchmen.

"The last years of Elizabeth's reign," writes G. J. Cuming, "saw the established Church in the ascendant, resting on the foundations that had been well and truly laid in the sixties and seventies. Papists and Puritans were both vigorously repressed, but neither were finally crushed. They could only await in patience the accession of a more favourably disposed monarch."[8]

The 1559 Book is more representative of Anglicanism than either of the earlier Books. It is also an integral part of the Elizabethan age, both as literature and as a book of devotion. "Shakespeare and Donne, Elizabeth and Essex, Raleigh and Jonson, Coke and Bacon, Hooker and Andrewes all worshiped with the Book of Common Prayer of 1559."[9]

CHAPTER IV

The Book of 1604

Elizabeth died and James I came to the throne on March 24, 1603. The very next month the Puritans presented him with a petition adopted by the general body of Puritans and signed by 1,000 ministers—the Millenary Petition—requesting a conference in order to deal with Puritan grievances including the services of the Church. James acceded to their request because of his own fondness for such a debate even though the conference was contrary to the wishes of the universities and the clergy generally. It was called to meet in the Fall but was then postponed until after Christmas. It met at Hampton Court on January 14, 16, and 18, 1604.

Regarding the Prayer Book, the petition listed "offences" which should be amended or removed or qualified, including the cross in Baptism, the square cap, the wedding ring, the word "priest," and bowing at the name of Jesus. The Puritans were also averse to Confirmation, to women administering private Baptism, and to the churching of women. They recommended that "examination" should go before Communion, that "the longsomeness of the service" be "abridged," and that "Church songs and music moderated." One suspects that they wished services to be abridged in order to allow more time for the sermon and extempore prayers, which would make the service even more "longsome."

The "Conference" was not really a conference. There was no discussion between Episcopal and Puritan divines. Rather it was first a meeting between the King and the Bishops for a day, then a meeting between the King and the Puritans on another day, and a third day's meeting at which the King presented his conclusions on the points debated.

After he heard the Puritans' objections to the 1559 Book, he made a few changes, but they were in the direction of catholicizing rather than puritanizing the Book. The principal changes were 1) adding "or Remission of Sins" to the title "Absolution," 2) adding prayers for members of the royal family to that for the King, 3) adding thanksgivings at the end of the Litany— For Rain, For Fair Weather, For Plenty, For Peace and Victory, and For Deliverance from Plague, 4) stating that private Baptism in houses is an exceptional practice and only to be performed by "a lawful minister," 5) adding "or Laying on of Hands upon children baptized, and able to render an account of their faith, according to the Catechism following," to the title "Confirmation," 6) adding a concluding portion on Sacraments to the Catechism. The Fourth or Jacobean Prayer Book was issued less than a month after the Hampton Court Conference. Its table of contents was identical to that of the 1559 Book save that there was a slight change in the order of some of the front-matter. In the Scripture appointed to be read, passages from the Apocrypha were omitted.

The liturgical changes resulting from the Hampton Court Conference were made by the King's letters patent (February 9, 1604) specifying the changes. Other than this only the canons needed attention. This was done that same year at the same time, consolidating the various Elizabethan directives. Those new canons also pronounced excommunication on those, whether Puritans or Romanists, who refused to use the Book.[1]

The major contribution of the Hampton Court Conference was unintentional and for the most part unwanted. It certainly was not listed in the Millenary Petition. At the conference Doctor Reynolds, the learned leader of the Puritan Party, proposed that there be a new translation of the Bible. His proposal was coolly received by his colleagues. After all, the Genevan Bible which was so popular with the laity was, through its notes and explanations, instilling Calvinistic interpretations and was to some degree responsible for the Puritan complexion of Parliament. The Puritans thought Reynolds' proposal was a strategic error. But it was received with enthusiasm by the King. His scholarly instincts were immediately aroused. He considered the Geneva Bible the worst of the English translations of Scripture. He also knew that Puritanism would continue to spread so long as the Geneva Bible was that of the people. He considered its "notes very partial, untrue, and seditious, and savouring too much of dangerous and traitorous conceits."[2]

The excellence of the translation of the Bible which James authorized as a result of the Hampton Court Conference is due to his common sense in appointing for the task men of learning and capacity regardless of their official position. There was something awesome and compelling about the production of that book. Dearmer describes it thus:

It was in this age of strife that the uniting spirit of the Bible for a while prevailed. Puritans and High Churchmen had the Scriptures in common, and did alike fervently believe in them: outside of the rooms in Oxford, Cambridge, and Westminster, where the forty-seven divines met, religious folk were maligning each other in brilliant, bitter, and abusive pamphlets; but within those learned conferences all hostilities were silenced, all differences ignored: men like Overall and the saintly Andrewes, on the one side, joined with Reynolds and Abbott, on the other; and the forty-seven worked in such singular harmony that it is impossible to distinguish between the three companies which assembled in three different places: the Authorized Version of the Bible reads like the work of one great man.[3]

The forty-seven scholars began their work in 1607 and produced the Authorized or, as it is called, the King James Version of the Bible in 1611.

The Puritans reacted determinedly against the 1604 Book. This first expressed itself in the publication of a critical examination of that Book. *Survey of the Book of Common Prayer* appeared in 1604. It pointed out the inconsistencies and superfluities of the 1604 Book in contrast to the Books of 1549 and 1552. This and other such writings were a formidable indictment. In the long view the ultimate value of their protests lay in the significance of the opposition they produced. That opposition is identified with Archbishop Laud and has had a profound influence on the worship, ceremonies, and arrangement of furniture in churches to this very day.

The Puritans vehemently objected to the use of the surplice. In contrast, the Laudians espoused outward adorning—lavish expenditure on copes (used only in cathedrals and college chapels), frontals, woodwork and fine bindings. In the practice of the Laudians ceremonies also, like outward adornments, became more elaborate. The Puritans objected to the cross in Baptism. The Laudians not only signed the infant with the cross but carried the newly baptized up to the altar. The Puritans disapproved of kneeling at communion. The Laudians made this but one gesture in a series of bowings and genuflections. Bishop Andrewes made a clear distinction between alms and oblations, having the congregation bring their oblations to the altar rail after the Creed and pronouncing a new set of sentences emphasizing offering before the people put their offerings into "poor man's chest."

The free-standing, unprotected Holy Table was subjected to unthinking mistreatment. People put their coats on it, dogs fouled its legs. Archbishop Laud placed the Holy Table against the east wall, fencing it with a rail, and thus causing communicants to come forward to receive. The canons directed that the Ante-Communion be read at the Altar, not in the reading-pew. Further directives stated that the Altar be covered with a silk or velvet carpet falling loose at the four corners. Richly carved altar-rails appeared and floors paved with marble in black and white squares. This was the typical Laudian sanctuary of the 1620s which is today taken for granted.

Archbishop Laud also left his mark on the liturgical history of Anglicanism through the Scottish Prayer Book of 1637. That Book was a beautiful baby albeit ill-conceived and untimely born. The story briefly is that the English Prayer Book, while used to some extent, was never popular in Scotland. In 1616 James I urged the Scottish bishops to introduce a new and acceptable service book. Little came of it because of the intense opposition aroused by James' insistence on kneeling at communion. But the project was taken up again by Charles I who urged it on his Archbishop of Canterbury, William Laud. Against his better judgment, Laud became involved, worked hard on the Book and is given credit for its significant and praiseworthy contents.

The Book which came out in the spring of 1637 was actually a revision of the English Prayer Book. It was doomed from the start. Because of mismanagement by the Scottish Bishops, in spite of Laud's repeated warnings, the Book of Canons came out first. This ordered the use of the Scottish Prayer Book. Because the clergy and the General Assembly were not consulted and their attitude seems hardly to have been considered, their negative reaction was predictable. The Book was fated to fail in spite of its excellence. It was silenced by a popular tumult as soon as the attempt was made to introduce it on July 23, 1637. So it can hardly be said to have been used at all.

While the Book was a failure, it was through no fault of its own. Moreover, its unpopularity and disuse were counterbalanced by its ultimate influence. A good deal of its amendment of the English Book of 1604 found its way into the 1662 Book. In addition, the changes which the English Book never adopted found their way via the Scottish Liturgy of 1764 into the Liturgy of the American Church. All of the American Prayer Books from 1789 to the present reflect dependence on this never-used Book.

In light of the Hampton Court Conference, the 1637 Book substitutes the Authorized Version of the Bible and does not contain readings from the Apocrypha. "Presbyter" replaces "priest" throughout. A thanksgiving for the departed which had been dropped in 1552 concludes the Prayer for the Whole State of Christ's Church. But so far as the American Prayer Book is concerned, the significant changes are in the Prayer of Consecration (now so named at Laud's suggestion). The *epiclesis* (invocation of the Holy Spirit) and the manual acts of 1549 are restored almost exactly as they were in that first Book. The Words of Institution are followed by the Memorial or Prayer of Oblation. Next follows the Lord's Prayer complete with doxology and introduced by "As our Lord Jesus Christ hath taught us, we are bold to say," which a Scottish Puritan divine called "that naughty preface." This is followed by the Prayer of Humble Access. The 1552 Words of Administration are dropped as being too Zwinglian, and upon reception the communicant responds, "Amen." G. J. Cuming calls the 1637 Book "the Laudian programme in full flower." It must be said, however, that while Laud defended the changes at his trial and had agreed to them as the Book was in the making, yet he disclaimed any responsibility for having originated them.[4]

The end of the Laudian era is sad. On March 1, 1641, the Archbishop was arrested and sent to the Tower of London. At the same time, a committee was appointed which demanded the abolition of altars, candlesticks, pictures and images, vestments and the Ornaments Rubric by which they "are now commanded," and many church ceremonies. Dearmer states that the bare condition of nineteenth-century churches was due far more to Puritan iconoclasts than to the Edwardian robbers. That bareness was the result of the destruction of the Prayer Book system.

On January 3, 1645, the very day on which William Laud was condemned to die, the Long Parliament by an Ordinance took away the Book of Common Prayer and established in its place the *Directory*, a manual of directions for the meager framework of Puritan worship. Again by Ordinance on August 23, 1645, the Long Parliament forbade the use of the Prayer Book in any "public place of worship or in any private place or family."

The Book of Common Prayer was officially dead.

CHAPTER V

The Book of 1662

Presbyterianism was the aggressively official religion of England for a decade and a half. It came to an end with the death of Oliver Cromwell, the Lord-Protector of England (in modern terms "the Dictator"), and the brief, feeble reign of his son, Richard. There was both general unrest and a widespread desire for the restoration of the Stuart dynasty. So negotiations were opened with Charles II who was in exile in The Netherlands.

The Presbyterians were determined to prevent the restitution of the Prayer Book. A deputation waited on Charles even before he left The Netherlands, seeking to dissuade him from using it. He received them politely and made every effort "to reduce them to such a temper as is consistent with the good of the Church." He also told them that he thought the Prayer Book "form of service the best in the world, and refused their request." Then he issued a declaration from Breda expressing concern for "a liberty to tender consciences ... in matters of religion."[1]

The King returned to London on May 29, 1660, and the people welcomed him jubilantly.

Undaunted by their initial rebuff, the Presbyterians began producing pamphlets arguing against the Prayer Book. They also submitted a list of grievances in writing to the King. Although they were answered by nine bishops, the Presbyterians were still not satisfied. In response to their continued pressure the King issued a "Declaration concerning Ecclesiastical Affairs" on October 25, 1660, stating that there would be a conference between the discordant parties, and then Convocation and Parliament would act.

On March 25, 1661, twelve bishops were appointed to meet with twelve Presbyterians. The twelve bishops represented the more conservative, pro-Prayer-Book-as-it-is point of view of the crown, and the Presbyterian party (which included some Puritan-minded bishops) wanted extensive revision. They were empowered "to advise upon and review the Book of Common Prayer; comparing the same with the most ancient Liturgies which have been used in the Church in the primitive and purest times." They were to hear objections, make "reasonable and necessary alterations and amendments therein as ... should be agreed upon to be needful or expedient for the giving satisfaction to tender consciences."[2] This commission was to have four months to do its work. The meetings were held at the Bishop of London's lodgings in the Savoy Hospital, hence the name, the Savoy Conference.

The commissioners included Bishops Cosin and Sanderson and among the Presbyterians Richard Baxter and Edward Reynolds, Bishop of Norwich. When the Conference opened, the Bishops said they were content with the Book as it stood (that is, the 1604 Book). The Presbyterians had a flood of objections to the Prayer Book, first orally stated and then reduced to writing. They were the familiar ones against which Puritans of earlier years had raised their voices: kneeling for communion, the sign of the cross in Baptism, Godparents speaking on behalf of infants, private Baptism (which they now wanted eliminated entirely), readings from the Apocrypha, the use of the word "priest," the ring in marriage, etc. And, of course, they wanted wide and unhindered use of extempore prayer. The Bishops conceded only 17 points out of 96. The Presbyterians tried in every way to gain their points, but to no avail. Their hostility to the Prayer Book was irreconcilable, though it only rested on small reasons, on misinterpreted phrases, or on doctrines opposed to Catholic truth. Their only significant gain was the substitution of the Authorized Version of the Bible throughout most of the Book. The few concessions made were not a bit satisfactory to them. The four months of the Savoy Conference were a tedious stand-off.

In the late Fall the whole business was concluded in Convocation in 22 days. Most of the work was apparently done in committees. Men like Bishops Sanderson, Cosin, and Wren played leading roles. The records of Convocation are unfortunately very brief. Apparently the greatest debate was on the age at which children should be confirmed! In late December,

1661, Convocation adopted the proposed Book and in January it went to Parliament. It was closer to the 1604 Book than either the Laudians or the Puritans would have desired. In Parliament it was neither discussed nor amended. The Act of Uniformity was debated, passed, and received royal assent on May 19, 1662. By the terms of the Act, the Book was to come into use not later than Saint Bartholomew's Day, August 24, of that same year. Neither the Laudians (High Churchmen) nor the Presbyterians (Puritans) had influenced the Book as much as they desired. The administration would have preferred to reissue the 1604 Book without any changes. However, some slight but hardly satisfactory concessions were made to both sides.

Here are the changes which distinguish this Book from the 1604 Book:

● The Epistles and Gospels were now from the Authorized Version of 1611 but the Psalter, the Ten Commandments, and excerpts in the Communion Service continued to be from the Great Bible of 1539.

● The Absolution in Morning and Evening Prayer was to be pronounced by the "Priest" instead of the "Minister."

● The Prayers for the King, Royal Family, Clergy and People, St. Chrysostom's Prayer and the Grace follow the Third Collect. This is the first time these prayers had all been part of the Daily Office. The Prayer for the King first appeared at the end of the Litany in 1559, and that for the Royal Family was added following it in the 1604 Book. The Prayer for Clergy and People, with venerable roots in the Gelasian Sacramentary, first appeared at the end of the 1544 Litany. The Prayer of St. Chrysostom, also of ancient origin, came into English as the concluding prayer of the Litany in 1544 and in the subsequent Books. Now it is also added here. The Grace which was inserted at the end of the Litany in 1559 is now added to the Office for the first time.

● Among the demands of the Presbyterians in the Savoy Conference was that there be prayers in contemporary English and that the congregational responses be removed from the Litany so that it would be one long prayer. While neither of these concerns is fully met, they are at least recognized in a minimal way.

The Prayer for all Conditions of Men and the General Thanksgiving are added to the Prayers and Thanksgivings as contemporary prayers. The former is a summary prayer which, according to the rubric that precedes it, is "to be used at such times when the Litany is not appointed to be said." In other words, it is to be said at Morning and Evening Prayer on such occasions. The petition for "all who profess and call themselves Christians" appearing in the Book so soon after the hard years under Cromwellian Presbyterianism sounds like the supercilious prayer of the Establishment for their late oppressors.

● Two interesting changes are made in the wording of Litany petitions. In the petition for the clergy, "Bishops, Priests, and Deacons" replaces "Bishops, Pastours, and Ministers." The latter had been in every version of the Litany since it first appeared in 1544. And to the petition beginning "From all sedition, privy conspiracy" are added the words "and rebellion," a reminder to this day of the Oliver Cromwell years.

● In the Communion Service, John Cosin's commemoration of the faithful departed is, to the horror of the Puritans, added to the end of the Prayer for the Church Militant. This brings the Book in line with both the Scotch Book of 1637 and the 1549 Book. (It had been omitted since 1552.) The "Black Rubric," which was added at the last minute in 1552 to insure that kneeling for reception did not imply veneration or indicate a doctrine of "real and essential presence there being of Christ's natural flesh and blood," is included in 1662 after having been omitted in 1559 and 1604. The crucial words, however, are changed to read, "no Adoration is intended ... unto any Corporal Presence of Christ's natural Flesh and Blood." So it excludes any doctrine of transubstantiation.

● The Catechism is printed separate from the Order of Confirmation.

● Bishop Cosin's translation of *Veni Creator* is added to the Ordering of Priests and Consecrating of Bishops in addition to Cranmer's translation which had been in these services since 1549.

● There are also numerous verbal changes throughout the Book, such as replacing "congregation" with the word "church." And some rubrics are made clearer for the sake of priests to whom the "customary manner" of former years is unknown. Also some new services are added which had become necessary to meet the circumstances of the times; for instance, a service of Adult Baptism to meet the case of converts from Anabaptism at home and from heathenism in "our plantations," and one for use at sea to meet the requirements of the rapidly increasing trade and navy of the country.

Great care was exercised by Convocation in making all of the above changes but little or no regard was paid to the objections of the Puritans. The Bishops rejected them as either "of dangerous consequence . . . or else of no consequence at all, but utterly frivolous and vain." So the main things to which the Puritans had been objecting for a hundred years—the use of the Apocrypha at certain times in the Daily Offices, the form of the Litany, the expressions in the services of Baptism, Marriage, and Burial, the vestments, the kneeling at Communion, the sign of the cross at Baptism, the ring at Marriage, the Absolution for the sick, and the declaration concerning the salvation of baptized infants—these were all retained by Convocation. And not just retained—with the passage of the Act of Uniformity in 1662 civil power went a step further, requiring ministers not only to adopt the new arrangements, but also to declare the unlawfulness of their past conduct and to submit to Episcopal ordination.

So with the 1662 Book the boundaries of exclusion set Presbyterianism definitely outside the Church of England.

Puritanism is too easily remembered for its narrow arrogance and negativity—the destruction of altars and ecclesiastical art, the blood of Archbishop Laud, the heavy hand of Oliver Cromwell. But there is another side. The destruction of ecclesiastical art and altars was not original with the Puritans. The small band of robbers in the reign of Edward VI differed no whit from the heavy-handed Puritans of the next century, save that they were motivated by avarice rather than fanaticism. But Puritanism also destroyed for us some ancient and deep-rooted evils, and helped us win the freedom to go back behind the traditions of men to the plain words and pure example of our

Lord Jesus Christ. This is a significant contribution, as was also their zeal for the Bible as they understood it.

The 1662 Book is still the official Book of the Church of England. When it is examined in perspective, its principal ancestor is the 1559 Book which was a revision of the Book of 1552. The changes made in 1604 were minimal and did not affect the tone of the Book. The changes of 1662 did alter its tone somewhat. But actually, as John Booty points out, the Elizabethan Book of 1559 is the norm, and in 1662 the tradition established a hundred years before won out over both the High Churchmen, such as John Cosin, and the Puritans, such as Richard Baxter.[3]

CHAPTER VI

The First American Prayer Book—1789

The strenuous and often fanatical efforts to revise the Prayer Book whether in a more Laudian (ceremonial) direction or in a more Puritan (Presbyterian) one lost some steam after England's Civil War and the adoption of the 1662 Book. People get tired. The fires of enthusiasm will take just so much stoking and then they tend to cool. The excesses of Calvinism, Romanism, Puritanism and Laudianism had had their day. The reaction resulted in a more moderate, less extreme position. The new science and the new philosophy of the period had their effect. Their adherents were called Latitudinarians.

Theirs was the Age of Reason, of Locke, of Newton, of Deism. The religious extremes of previous decades were repugnant to them. They eschewed both Romanism and Calvinism, and as men of their times they sought to minister to the Age of Reason. So the emphasis was on common sense and reason. Scripture was looked upon as the basis of Christian faith and practice, and they placed less emphasis upon tradition than had the Laudians. The accent was on morality and good works, rather than theology. They had a less exalted view of the episcopacy and the sacraments than the Laudians; polity and ceremonial were of secondary importance. The doctrinal temper of the age tended toward Deism and Unitarianism.

Beyond 1662 there were still spurts of concern for revision and greater inclusiveness, but the general disposition of the times dampened any such ardor. Two abortive attempts were made in the latter part of the seventeenth century to reach a comprehensiveness which would embrace the Presbyterians. The first was led by John Wilkins, Bishop of Chester and brother-in-law of Cromwell, in 1668. The second came shortly after William and Mary succeeded James II in 1688. Nothing came of either.

In another way the forced departure of James II from the throne did lie behind a bit of the Prayer Book's story. A number of clergy—some four hundred, including nine bishops and even Sancroft of Canterbury—could not bring themselves to give their allegiance to the new monarchs. On August 1, 1689, all of these non-juror clergy were suspended. A number of Scottish bishops and clergy took the same stance. This outlawed, non-juror Anglican Church which refused to give allegiance to the Crown was a century later to consecrate the first American Bishop, Samuel Seabury of Connecticut.

During the next 100 years, there were numerous Latitudinarian proposals for Prayer Book revision. These unofficial growing pains did not overturn the official status of the 1662 Book. There were also some developments related to the Scottish Book of 1637. Beginning in 1722, the first of several "Wee Bookies" appeared. It was a reprint of the Scottish rite of 1637 and was apparently intended to be used in conjunction with the other offices of the English Book of 1662. The most important of these Wee Bookies appeared in 1764 and, as we shall see, cast its significant shadow on the American Prayer Book.

The events of July 4, 1776, produced the first American change in the Book of Common Prayer—petitions for the King and royal family were immediately deleted in many churches. A few years later, after the peace had been signed, that which had been the Church of England in the Colonies began to forge its new identity.

The name "Protestant Episcopal" evolved. The name was indicative of the Church American Anglicans were setting themselves to establish. *Protestant* meant a non-Roman catholic church and *episcopal* meant that bishops were integral to its structure. Before long the term, "a protestant episcopal church," which was first used in Maryland as merely a description of this Amercian Church, had become "The Protestant Episcopal Church," the borning of a new branch of the Anglican Church which intended to be separate from, yet ongoing with, the Mother Church. For this to become a reality, the American Church had to acquire bishops properly consecrated by bishops in apostolic succession, and have its own liturgy.

Two separate movements toward accomplishing these objectives began almost as soon as peace had been declared. First, Connecticut elected Samuel Seabury bishop and sent him to England for consecration. Second, two years later in 1786 a convention of the "southern states" (so-called because the New England states were not represented) produced a proposed Prayer Book for the American Church. The events that took place in New England and in the southern states are separate but related strands, sometimes touching, sometimes apart, which in 1789 became interwoven to produce the first American Prayer Book. Look first at the New England strand during the years 1785 and 1786.

In November, 1784, Seabury was consecrated by the Non-Juror Bishops of Scotland. The reason he went to Scotland for consecration was that in the English Service one had to give one's allegiance to the Crown, which, obviously, he could not do. Of course the Non-Jurors, as we have seen, had no such requirement, so Seabury turned to them for consecration. The Non-Juror Communion Service which was used at his consecration was the generally accepted Scottish Office—the 1764 revision of the service in the Scottish Book of 1637. The day after his consecration Seabury and his consecrators signed a concordat which contained these gentle words:

> ... the Scottish Bishops ... ardently wishing that Bishop Seabury would endeavor all he can, consistently with peace and prudence, to make the celebration of this venerable mystery conformable to ... the pattern the Church of Scotland has copied after in her Communion Service. ... Bishop Seabury ... agrees to take a serious view of the Communion Office recommended by them ... to give his sanction to it, and by gentle methods of argument and persuasion, to endeavor ... to introduce it by degrees into practice. ...[1]

The new Bishop Seabury first met with the convocation of his clergy at Middletown, Connecticut, August 2–5, 1785. In his lengthy charge he urged them to preach pure doctrine, to exercise care in administering Holy Orders, and to stress Confirmation, but there was no mention of his concordat with the Scottish Bishops. A committee was appointed to consider changes in the liturgy necessitated by the political situation. Neither the minutes nor any of the addresses contain any mention of Seabury's concordat with the Scottish Bishops. Moreover, the proposed alterations to the Prayer Book, presented by Seabury himself before the meeting ended completely ignored the concordat.

"The Church people of Connecticut," Seabury wrote to Samuel Parker several months later, "were much alarmed at the thought of any considerable alteration being made in the Prayer Book."[2] And it appears that the Bishop of Connecticut was reluctant to stand up to his people's opposition to change. The changes in the liturgy in Connecticut and subsequently in Massachusetts were chiefly those necessitated by the political changes, and the general substance of all their revisions reflected the views of the English Latitudinarians contained in some of the rather widely-read books on Prayer Book revision which had appeared in England earlier in the century.[3]

It was a whole year later (September 22, 1786) before Seabury presented what came to be called the "Bishop Seabury Communion Service" to the Connecticut clergy, recommending its use. That service was the Scottish Service of 1764 which had been used at his consecration. But while the Bishop of Connecticut was in correspondence with Dr. (later Bishop) White prior to the "southern states" Convention in 1785 regarding Prayer Book revision, he only mentioned "such alternations as have been thought necessary to accommodate our Liturgy to the Civil Constitution of this State." There was no mention of his concordat with the Scottish Bishops.

The proposed Book of 1786 which the "southern states" convention adopted was basically the 1662 Book with revisions similar to many of the Latitudinarian suggestions published in England in the eighteenth century. Its most conspicuous changes from the 1662 Book were the omission of the Nicene and Athanasian Creeds and the deletion of the words "He descended into hell" from the Apostles' Creed. It is interesting to note that without any encouragement from Seabury there is evidence of Scottish influence on that book. Many of the Scottish clergy in the States were surely familiar with the Wee Bookies. Dr. William Smith, who was active in the organization of the Church in Maryland and a leader in the "southern states" Convention, was one of them. Among the minimal changes in the Proposed Book which point to familiarity with the Scottish Book of 1764 was the placing of the Collects, Epistles, and Gospels after the

Communion Service instead of before it as in the 1662 Book.

The Proposed Book of 1786 was not well received. William White's Vestry at the United Church of Christ and St. Peter's, Philadelphia, stood behind him and voted immediately "that the new Books of common prayer be used . . . until further order shall be taken. . . ." The state conventions of Virginia and Maryland voted to use the book. But David Griffith of Virginia repeatedly reported to White that book sales were minimal. And while William Smith of Maryland wrote White for more copies, he reported that "some old persons do not show much desire to exchange the old for the new book." Thomas Claggett, who was to become the first Bishop of Maryland six years later, reported that "the people of this congregation (I mean ye Church's real Friends, ye communicants) universally disapprove of ye new Book. . . ."

The principal objection among those who approached the matter canonically was that the revision had been done by the "southern states" Convention without the sanction of a bishop; they thought that all alterations of the liturgy were the business of bishops. The New York and the New Jersey Conventions shared this view. In New Jersey they were quite militant about it and in February, two months before the Proposed Book even appeared in print, began marshalling forces to protest the action of the Philadelphia Convention. This was also Bishop Seabury's primary objection to the Book. He thus found it an obstacle to the unification of the Church in New England with the Church in the "southern states." Among the Connecticut clergy, another objectionable feature of the Proposed Book was that it contained thirty-one selections of Psalms for use throughout the month. Many of these selections were made up of portions of several Psalms rather than entire Psalms taken right from the Bible.

Still other reactions were of a piece with feelings of church people about Prayer Book revision every time it takes place. The Reverend Henry Purcell wrote to White, "I am sorry to acquaint you that the Reform does not improve on the Affections of the People here, but is rather received with fresh Tokens of Disgust, the more it is used, & searched into. . . ." And the Reverend Jeremiah Leaming of Connecticut, a respected Church leader who had the best interests of the Church at heart, wrote to Abraham Beach of New Jersey, "I suppose it will be impossible to bring the members of our church in this state, to lay aside the English prayer book, and receive the new one. Would there be any inconsistency in our uniting with the Southern Churches, although we continue to use the old prayer book?"

There was also the widespread impression that the Proposed Book was the final and unalterable American Prayer Book. This produced very negative reactions. Years later in his *Memoirs* Bishop White attributed this impression to the fact that the Book was used in Christ Church, Philadelphia, "on the occasion of Dr. Smith's sermon, at the conclusion of the session of the convention. This helped to confirm the opinion, of its being to be introduced [*sic*] with a high hand."[4] In an effort to counteract this widespread misconception, the "southern states" Convention of July 1786, three months after the Book first went into circulation, declared by resolution:

Our Book is only a Proposal . . . we have not established it, nor do we consider ourselves as having Authority so to do in the Churches of any of these States, 'till they are fully organized and have their Bishops in Council and Government with them.[5]

The English Bishops to whom the churches of the "southern states" looked for the consecration of their bishops took a dim view of what the Americans had done to the Creeds:

. . . we cannot help being afraid . . . lest we should be the instrument of establishing an Ecclesiastical system which will be called a branch of the Church of England, but afterwards may appear to have departed from it essentially, either in doctrine or in discipline.

In spite of their reservations, they had "prepared a Bill for conveying to us the powers necessary" to consecrate the American Bishops. At the same time they gently urged that the Apostles' Creed be restored "to its integrity," and that the two other Creeds be included for "discretional" use.[6] The "southern states" responded to this communication at the second session of their 1786 Convention (October 10–11) by restoring both the Nicene Creed and permissive use of the descent-into-hell clause of the Apostles' Creed. This action received the approval of the English Bishops and cleared the way for White of

Pennsylvania and Provoost of New York to sail to England the next month for episcopal consecration.

The "southern states" convened their next convention on July 28, 1789. In order to embrace the Church in New England and bring about a union of the Episcopal Church in all of the United States, they renounced any commitment to the Proposed Book. The consequence of this action was that on September 29, 1789, the first General Convention of the Protestant Episcopal Church met in Philadelphia. Its members met as two houses—the House of Bishops, composed of Bishops Seabury and White (Provoost was ill and absent), and the House of Deputies, which included for the first time delegates representing Connecticut Massachusetts, and New Hampshire.

Those who attended were certainly a diverse assembly. They included John Jay, president of the First Continental Congress; John Page, Revolutionary leader, friend of Thomas Jefferson and later Governor of Virginia; David Griffith, former Chaplain in the Continental Line, friend of Washington and Lafayette; and William White, chaplain to Congress during the Revolution. At the other political extreme were Samuel Seabury, ardent Tory pamphleteer and British chaplain, and among the other clergy, Abraham Beach and Abraham Jarvis, who had been serious Tories and had little respect for the patriots who by their support of the Revolution had violated their oath of loyalty to the Crown. From an ecclesiastical point of view there were some who doubted the validity of Seabury's Non-Juror consecration. In that company the tensions were great. In addition, those in positions of power were difficult to deal with, and some of them could not get along with certain others. The possibility that this band of apparent irreconcilables might reach any consensus looked dim. But the seemingly impossible was brought about by the patience and statesmanship of those in key positions, principally William White and William Smith. Moreover, it was accomplished without breaking off communion with the Church of England.

The diversity of that assembly of churchmen in Philadelphia was also present in their thinking as to what should constitute their revision of the Prayer Book. Some thought it was only necessary to make those revisions of the 1662 Book which the political situation dictated. Some wanted to eliminate certain elements which had been distasteful to the Puritans from the early years. Still others felt the need to add supplementary offices. Many were quite sympathetic with certain Latitudinarian proposals which would eliminate references to the Trinity and address all prayers to the Father. Finally, there were several who thought the Book should be enriched along Non-Juror Scottish and Eastern lines. This last emphasis was to some degree related to the ardor of a younger William Smith (not to be confused with Dr. William Smith, Bishop White's friend and colleague), who had once served a church in Maryland and was now in Newport, Rhode Island. Young Smith was strongly influenced by Thomas Rattray's *The Ancient Liturgy of the Church of Jerusalem* (1744), which was the first serious Anglican study in comparative liturgies. It included "An Office for the Sacrifice of the Holy Eucharist." Marion Hatchett says that this work was in the hands of some of the delegates to that General Convention and that young Smith actively urged consideration of it in correspondence with Dr. Smith and a number of other delegates.[7]

So this was the heterogeneous assembly of strong-willed churchmen who sat down together to forge the first American revision of the Book of Common Prayer. It took them ten days. The principal subjects of difference between the two Houses were the retention of the Athanasian Creed, the descent-into-hell clause in the Apostles' Creed, and the use of the Psalter. Bishop Seabury wanted to retain the Athanasian Creed for optional use; the deputies were firmly against it. The descent-into-hell clause was included in the Apostles' Creed, but, because the words were considered to be of uncertain meaning, a rubric was added explaining them as "He went into the place of departed spirits." (That rubric also appeared in the revisions of 1892 and 1928.) The Selection of Psalms was strongly favored by the deputies. This was a schedule of appointed Psalms for each day of the month. Many of the selections contained verses from several Psalms. At first the bishops did not agree to their inclusion. However, when the selections were limited to eight which might be used at the discretion of the minister, the Bishops acquiesced and added two.

The most significant difference between the first American Book and the 1662 Book is the Prayer of Consecration in the

Holy Communion. Bishop Seabury had brought to Philadelphia his notebook containing the Communion rite he had introduced in Connecticut in 1786. The Maryland and Pennsylvania state conventions of 1786 had also made revisions along Scottish lines. The Prayer of Consecration as finally phrased was that in Bishop Seabury's notebook, with the latter half of the Invocation revised in the light of the proposals of the Maryland and Pennsylvania deputies. It was not at all certain that this radical change from the 1662 rite would pass the House of Deputies and be adopted. Here is a dramatic account of how that came about as told by Thomas W. Coit who supposedly received it from Samuel Farmar Jarvis, whose father, Abraham Jarvis, attended the Convention. Having explained that Dr. William Smith, President of the House of Deputies, was aware of the opposition to the proposed Prayer of Consecration, Jarvis reports that this is what Smith did:

He rose in his place, and, exclaiming, "Hear—(Smith was a born Scotsman, pronouncing it *Heyre*)—before ye judge," began to read. Dr. Smith was a superb reader and withal had just enough of a Scotch brogue to make his tones more musical and his emphasis more thrilling. He soon caught attention, and read his paper through without a single interruption, his hearers becoming more and more absorbed and charmed. When he had finished, the new office was accepted with acclamations.

The revised form of the Eucharistic Prayer is usually thought to be the major improvement of the American Book over its 1662 English predecessor. Bishop Seabury has usually been given the credit for bringing this about. Marion Hatchett observes that "it seems highly doubtful that this prayer would have made its way into the book on his recommendation." He was only one of several agents who brought it about acting in concert, for we must not forget the energetic and roving young William Smith who used the Scottish prayer in Pennsylvania, Maryland, and Rhode Island, and who wrote the delegates to the 1789 Convention about the Scottish prayer and its origin. Also, the Maryland and Pennsylvania State Conventions had both proposed revisions along Scottish lines. Then Dr. William Smith so ably presented it in the House of Deputies, and Bishop White's acceptance of it certainly carried considerable weight. Samuel Parker of Boston, who spoke highly of the Scottish prayer, should probably be included, for he was much respected.

In addition, it must be remembered that Seabury had met strong
resistance when he sought to introduce the Scottish Communion
Service in Connecticut. Indeed, one account we have of the
September, 1786, meeting of Connecticut clergy states that Seabury "hath made *an attempt* to alter the Communion Service, ...
But it was with *a noble spirit rejected,* when palmed upon the
Clergy by *dint of Episcopal Supremacy.*" There may well have
been a more widespread use of the Eucharistic Prayer based on
the earlier Scottish rite in Maryland and Pennsylvania than
was found in Connecticut. Hatchett looks at all of these factors
and concludes that "though Seabury may have influenced the
form which the final revision took, he could not single-handedly
have carried the day for it and should not be given over-much
credit." So far as we know, he never mentioned his concordat
with the Scottish bishops, and that document was not published
in the United States until 1822, 26 years after his death.[8]

The book produced by the General Convention of 1789 appeared in 1790. It bore the title which has graced the title page
of every American revision since: *The Book of Common Prayer,
and Administration of the Sacraments, and Other Rites and Ceremonies of the Church, According to the Use of the Protestant
Episcopal Church in the United States of America: together with
the Psalter, or Psalms of David.*

This is the extent and order of its contents:

1. The Ratification of the book of Common Prayer.

2. The Preface.

3. The Order how the Psalter is appointed to be read.

4. The Order how the Rest of the Holy Scripture is ap-
    pointed to be read.

5. Tables of Lessons of Holy Scripture, to be read at Morn-
    ing and Evening Prayer, throughout the Year.

6. The Calendar.

7. Tables and Rules for the Moveable and Immoveable
    Feasts, together with the Days of Fasting, and Abstinence
    throughout the Year.

8. Tables for finding the Holy-Days.

9. The Order of Daily Morning Prayer.

10. The Order of Daily Evening Prayer.
The Litany (not mentioned in the original Table of Contents).

11. Prayers and Thanksgivings upon several Occasions, to be used before the two final Prayers of Morning and Evening Service.

12. The Collects, Epistles, and Gospels, to be used throughout the Year.

13. The Order for the Administration of the Lord's Supper, or Holy Communion.

14. The Ministration of Public Baptism of Infants, to be used in the Church.

15. The Ministration of Private Baptism of Children, in Houses.

16. The Ministration of Baptism to such as are of Riper Years, and able to answer for themselves.

17. A Catechism: that is to say, an Instruction to be learned by every Person before he be brought to be confirmed by the Bishop.

18. The Order of Confirmation, or Laying on of Hands upon those that are Baptized, and come to Years of Discretion.

19. The Form of Solemnization of Matrimony.

20. The Order for the Visitation of the Sick.

21. The Communion of the Sick.

22. The Order for the Burial of the Dead.

23. The Thanksgiving of Women after Child-Birth; commonly called the Churching of Women.

24. Forms of Prayer to be used at Sea.

25. A Form of Prayer for the Visitation of Prisoners.

26. A Form of Prayer and Thanksgiving to Almighty God, for the Fruits of the Earth, and all the other Blessings of his merciful Providence.

27. Forms of Prayer to be used in Families.

28. Selections of Psalms, to be used instead of the Psalms for the Day, at the Discretion of the Minister.

29.   The Psalter, or Psalms of David.

As one leafs through the book here are some of the things which catch the eye:

● The Preface is simply that of the 1786 Proposed Book condensed.

● In Morning and Evening Prayer, the words "on earth" in the Lord's Prayer have replaced "in earth." Indeed, throughout the book language is modernized: for example, "who" for "which" and "that" referring to persons; "which" for "that" referring to things; "are" for "be"; "Jesus" for "Jesu"; "forgotten" for "forgot," and others. The *Venite* is composed of parts of Psalms 95 and 96 rather than being all of Psalm 95. The *Benedicite* is an alternate to the *Te Deum* as in the 1662 Book. The *Benedictus* is an alternate to the *Jubilate Deo*, but there are only four verses. In Evening Prayer both the *Magnificat* and the *Nunc dimittis* are omitted. In the Apostles' Creed, "again" is omitted from the clause "The third day he rose from the dead." And while "He descended into hell" has been restored, it is in italics and brackets. (The 1792 Convention corrected this.) In the 1662 Book the *Kyrie* and Lord's Prayer followed the Creed. These are omitted. There is no provision for an anthem following the Third Collect as there is in the 1662 Book. And for the first time the prayer For All Conditions of Men and A General Thanksgiving are printed in Morning and Evening Prayer.

● The rubric at the beginning of the Litany reads, "To be used after Morning Service, on Sundays, Wednesdays, and Fridays."

● The section of Prayers and Thanksgivings has been considerably expanded. It now includes prayers for Congress, For Meetings and Conventions, In a Time of Great Sickness and Mortality, For a Sick Person, For a Sick Child, For a Person Going to Sea, For a Person under Affliction, and For Malefactors. There are also new thanksgivings For a Woman After Child-Birth, For Recovery from Sickness, For a Child's Recovery, and For Safe Return from Sea.

● The Holy Communion Service contains several variations from the 1662 Book in addition to the Prayer of Consecration which we have already examined. The initial rubric directs that when the service begins the Minister stand "at the north side of the

Table [this was later changed to "standing at the right side"], or where Morning and Evening Prayer are appointed to be said." In eighteenth-century churches Morning Prayer was read from the triple-decker pulpit in the middle of the north wall. The chancel was on the east wall. The tone of the rubric suggests that Ante-Communion was customarily used with Morning Prayer. The Summary of the Law has been added and may be said following the Decalogue. The *Gloria tibi*—"Glory be to thee, O Lord"—follows the announcement of the Gospel. It had been included in the 1549 service but was then dropped in 1552 and did not appear again until the Scottish Book of 1637. The title of the Prayer for the Whole State of Christ's Church omits the words "here on earth," and the Invitation replaces the archaic "meekly kneeling upon your knees" with the simple "devoutly kneeling." A hymn is ordered following the Prayer of Consecration, and a hymn may be substituted for the *Gloria in excelsis*. At the end of the service the "Black Rubric" is omitted.

● The Collects, Epistles, and Gospels are obviously based on the Proposed Book of 1786.

● The Proposed Book also influences the Occasional Offices. The sign of the cross may be omitted in Baptism. However, the emphasis on regeneration which was omitted from the Proposed Book is restored in its 1662 form. Confirmation is the 1662 service with a few verbal changes from the Proposed Book. Marriage is the Proposed Book revision of the 1662 service. Burial is based on that service in the Proposed Book.

● A notable omission is that there is no notice taken of July the Fourth—no prayer, no propers, no service—as in the Proposed Book. The war was too recent. The subject was too controversial for the delegates to handle. However, a few years later the bishops of New York and New Jersey authorized appropriate services for the occasion based upon the service in the Proposed Book.

While the Proposed Book of 1786 was immensely unpopular and while the last convention of the "southern states" disavowed any allegiance to it, it is not true, as some scholars suggest, that it did not play a part in the work of the 1789 Convention. A close analysis of the 1789 Book reveals that the Preface, Lectionary, Prayers and Thanksgivings, and the revision of almost every one of the Occasional Offices is the version of the Proposed Book.

The spirit of the 1789 Convention was one of brotherly concern, and it was evident that for those participating, the interest and welfare of the whole Church was primary. Bishop Seabury might have come to Philadelphia with a chip on his shoulder, but he did not. Years later, Bishop White remembered "especially the Christian temper which he manifested all along." Another conciliatory person was Samuel Parker of Boston. He suggested that "the proceedings be held without any reference to that . . . proposed in 1785." He was probably doing this out of deference to the Connecticut delegates, for he himself was not averse to some of its changes. Perhaps the most striking example of the generous spirit of those who forged the first American Prayer Book comes not from this convention but from the Convention of 1786. Bishop White had wished to eliminate the July the Fourth service of thanksgiving for civil liberty because it would be an affront to Loyalist clergy and others. He was, however, over-ridden. Later he learned that the service had been composed by Dr. William Smith, himself a staunch Loyalist.[9] That same generous-spirited Dr. Smith was the president of the House of Deputies in 1789.

The Prayer Book which finally passed the 1789 Convention was required to be used from and after the first day of October in the following year.

The editorial committee charged with publishing the book finally got it into the hands of the printer on January 16, 1790. Its members attempted to be faithful to their instructions, but they made one monumental blunder. The Deputies had directed that the descent-into-hell clause be printed in a distinctive manner with a rubric permitting its omission or words of substitution. The Bishops simply desired a rubric clarifying its meaning—"to be the state of the dead, generally." Through some mistake these two proposals were not reconciled by General Convention. The committee printed the words in italics, put them in brackets, and failed to supply the rubric giving explanatory words which might be substituted. This raised a multitude of New England hackles. Seabury objected: "I shall, on that account, think myself at perfect liberty to reject the whole book," he wrote White. This blunder and a change regarding the required prayers in the Morning Prayer provided the Bishop of Connecticut with an excuse for disassociating himself from the book if, because of the negative reaction of his people, that seemed expedient.

But the dust clouds soon settled and temperatures went down, even in Connecticut, and the reaction to the book was generally favorable. In September, 1790, Seabury again wrote to White:

... there will be some difficulty in bringing our book into common use in this State, though, I flatter myself, it will be done, if not at once, yet gradually in the course of a year or two.

He goes on to list the local objections to the book: omission of the Athanasian Creed, "the disfiguring of the Apostles' Creed," omission of the Commination Office (a service "Denouncing of God's Anger and Judgement against Sinners ... to be used on the first day of Lent"), the rubric permitting the omission of the sign of the cross in Baptism, and the use of the Burial Office for unbaptized children. A month later the clergy of Connecticut confirmed "the doings of our Proctors in General Convention at Philadelphia." There was only one negative vote—James Sayre walked out of the meeting. At that same meeting they agreed to use the book in a uniform fashion and also "that we approach as near the Old Liturgy, as a compliance with the Rubrics of the *New* will allow."

Shortly after the convention Samuel Parker wrote to Bishop White from Boston, "I find my Constituents are generally well pleased with the Account I have given of the Proceedings of the Convention. . . ." This seems to have been the general reaction, although there were some negative feelings and some reservations.

The New York state convention deplored the omission of the Articles of Religion and instructed their delegates to the next General Convention to seek their restoration.

The New Jersey state convention, always quick to react, voted unanimously before the book even came off the press, that they were bound by the proceedings of their delegates at General Convention. There was some objection in that state when the book came out to the omission of the Articles of Religion and the Ordinal. Neither of these had been taken up at the 1789 Convention; they were probably considered future agenda items.

There does not appear to have been any widespread, concerted opposition to the book. However, there were some unreconcilable individuals. James Sayre, who walked out of the meeting of Connecticut clergy, was one. He was a stubborn Scotsman, as likely to bend as an icicle. At Newport, Rhode Island, in the late 1780s, he had resisted the use of the Boston Proposals even though they had been in use in that congregation since 1785. This became part of the cause for his leaving. He went to Stratford, Connecticut, where he resisted the use of the 1789 Book, actually refusing to communicate those who did use it. Finally Bishop Seabury suspended him from performing any "Ecclesiastical Offices" of the church "until he shall by repentance and reformation of his conduct be qualified for, and shall be restored to its Peace and Communion." The stiff-necked old Scot never recanted.

Another person who found himself out of step with liturgical change was Dr. Benjamin Rush, a Philadelphia physician and professor and a signer of the Declaration of Independence, who was only confirmed two years before the Book was published. He wrote to John Adams, "The Episcopal Church at that time divested itself of many of its absurdities in doctrine and worship," but "by their restoration of Bishop Seabury, I was thrown out of its pale." In his autobiography he later wrote:

In consequence of an alteration made in the forms of Baptism and the communion service, the former admitting infant regeneration, and the latter favouring transubstantiation, I declined after a year or two communing in the church, and had my children baptized by Presbyterian ministers.[10]

Another Connecticut Scotsman whose strong feelings were tempered with a redeeming bit of twinkle was the Reverend Ebenezer Dibblee. Hardly had the delegates returned from the 1789 Convention before he wrote Samuel Peters in England, "I am told, mutilations, omissions and alterations in our Service, are inconsiderable & of no importance ... Poor Athanasius is beheaded, his Creed condemned as heretical." But after the book came out he avoided its use. In February, 1792, Bishop

Seabury wrote him, "If you cannot use the book with a good conscience, I have not a word to say to prevail on you to do so.... But ... sooner or later [your people] will suffer by your refusal." Evidently the old fellow came around, but grudgingly. The next year he again wrote his English friend Peters, "The new Service is generally adopted in the States, & complied with for peace & unity sake; altho the omissions & verbal alterations, will never by agreeable to the old Tory Churchmen...."

But on the whole the book was accepted with relatively little opposition. People realized that because of the political changes some revision of the Prayer Book was inevitable. The Proposed Book of 1786 had been too radical a departure from the familiar 1662 Book. There was a general disposition to go along with the work of General Convention, now that the American Church was properly established with its own House of Bishops. Actually, when the book is viewed alongside the other revisions of the period, it is both restrained and conservative. And Marion Hatchett's analysis of its quality can make us rather proud of this accomplishment of our ecclesiastical forebears:

The judgment of the American Episcopal Church, of Anglicanism, and of the other communions has seemed to be that the first American revisers did a better job than they could have guessed in holding fast to what was of value in the old and in winnowing out the chaff from the wheat among the proposals which were before them.[11]

CHAPTER VII

The Book of 1892

The 1792 General Convention made several slight tidying-up changes in the new American Book authorized three years before. The descent-into-hell clause in the Apostles' Creed was printed so as not to give offense—no longer in italics, and without the brackets. However, the rubric gave permission to omit it or to substitute the words "He went into the place of departed spirits." In Confirmation at the laying-on-of-hands, the word "hand" which had been the use in every Book from 1549, was changed to "hands." The rubric in Morning Prayer directing that the Litany is to follow was placed by the editorial committee of 1789 after the Prayer for the President rather than after the Third Collect. Hence the Prayer for the President was always obligatory. This caused some rumblings of disapproval. The 1792 Convention, however, allowed it to stand. There were no other changes of any great moment.

During the next thirty years there were several changes and additions which affected the Book. The 1808 Convention changed the Constitution of the Church so as to require two successive General Conventions to make any change in the Prayer Book. At that same Convention an "Office of Institution of Ministers," which had been under discussion at several previous General Conventions, was added to the Book. The 1820 Convention bound the Ordinal in with the Prayer Book. The 1832 and 1835 Conventions made numerous changes. In the Communion Service the rubric which stated that the Minister was "standing at the north side of the Table" was changed to read "standing at the right side of the Table." "A Form for the Consecration of a Church or Chapel" became part of the Book. The Articles of Religion had been incorporated into the Book in 1801. They had undergone some changes since and finally, in 1835, they

59

reached the form in which they are now familiar to us. And
over 1,700 corrections of punctuation, capitalization, typography
and the like were made.

In all of this time there was no real revision of the Prayer
Book. In 1826 Bishop Hobart did propose these changes:

● That the minister be allowed to use any Psalm or Psalms in
place of those appointed.

●That the minister be allowed to shorten the lections for Sundays
and Holy Days or to make substitutions for the appointed
lections for other days.

● An alternative Preface and an alternative first prayer for the
Confirmation Rite.

● A substitute rubric to be printed after the Communion Service, to make it plain that Ante-Communion is to be said when
there is a Sermon or Communion as well as when there is no
Sermon or Communion.

However, Hobart himself removed these from consideration at
the next Convention because "under existing circumstances it
is not expedient. . . ."

But the fact that there was no serious move to revise the
Prayer Book during the major part of the nineteenth century
does not mean that churchmen were not "tossed to and fro and
carried about with every kind of doctrine, by the cunning of
men, by their craftiness in deceitful wiles" (Eph. 4:14). That
century had more than its share of new movements which might
have been schismatic or at least disruptive, and of unsettling
events. Marion Hatchett's list of them is positively frightening—
"Hobartianism, Evangelicalism, Tractarianism, Ultramontanism,
evolutionary science and philosophy, Higher Criticism, feelings
of insecurity in the face of the large scale immigration of Roman
Catholics, the disruption of North and South, Ritualism, and
changes in taste and fashion in regard to church architecture,
music, and ceremonial. . . ."[1] Possibly there were no determined
moves toward revision because of the fear that one's opponent
of whatever stripe might gain some undesirable victory in the
process. But there was also the perhaps unspoken security of
having the Book of Common Prayer as a buoy in the midst of
a storm of change. Henry Francis Lyte composed his familiar

hymn "Abide With Me" during this century. No doubt many misappropriated his words to the Prayer Book: "Change and decay in all around I see; / O thou who changest not, abide with me." Here was a benchmark to which the extremists could be recalled. Here was a yardstick against which those who aspired to refashion the Church's ways could measure themselves.

Then, just as a certain early lightness presages the dawn, the "Muhlenberg Memorial," presented to the General Convention of 1853, caused stirrings which ultimately resulted in a revision of the Prayer Book forty years later. Doctor William Augustus Muhlenberg and other forward-looking churchmen sought a relaxation of obligatory rubrics and advocated greater flexibility and variety in liturgical use. All that apparently came of the consideration of the Muhlenberg Memorial initially was that three years later the Bishops declared that Morning Prayer, the Litany, and Holy Communion were three separate services, and that "under the advice of the Bishop" they might be used separately. "In point of fact," stated *The Churchman* almost thirty years later, "everything that has characterized the progress of the Church since 1853 may be traced to the Muhlenberg Memorial."[2]

The matter of more liberty in public worship came up at one General Convention after another—1868, 1871, 1874, 1877. At the 1877 Convention a breach was made in the solid unchangeable masonry of the century-old Book—the new English Lectionary of 1871, which included Apocryphal readings, was approved for permissive use, but only for the next three years. Also at that Convention, Doctor William Reed Huntington moved that a Joint Committee be appointed to consider

what changes, if any, are needed in the rubrics of the Book of Common Prayer to remove difficulties of interpretation, to amend the Lectionary, and to provide by abbreviation or otherwise for the better adaption of the services of the Church to the wants of all sorts and conditions of men.

But the General Convention was not prepared to consider the possibility of changing the Prayer Book, however slight and conservative that change might be. Huntington's motion was tabled.

Three years later at the 1880 Convention, the persistent Doctor

Huntington tried again; this time his resolution had a certain sentimental appeal. He proposed a Joint Committee to consider

whether in view of the fact that this Church is soon to enter upon the second century of its organized existence in this country, the changed conditions of national life do not demand certain alterations in the Book of Common Prayer, in the direction of Liturgical enrichment and increased flexibility of use.

A Joint Committee, consisting of seven bishops, seven presbyters and seven laymen, was appointed and ordered to report to the Convention of 1883.

The members of the Committee, a majority of whom had not even voted in favor of Huntington's resolution, met shortly after the adjournment of General Convention. It was quite obvious that initially they did not conceive of their task as extending beyond suggesting rubrical changes which would make shorter services possible. As it turned out, all of them did not have so limited a view of their commission, nor did some others throughout the Church. The Convention had hardly adjourned before the editor of *The Churchman* was calling for "tentative services . . . authorized by the Church for trial."[3]

The report of the Joint Committee was ready in the Spring of 1883 in time for deputies and bishops to study it before General Convention convened in the Fall. To the actual report was attached a full volume showing what the Prayer Book would be like should the proposals of the Committee be adopted. In the report it was referred to as "the book annexed." That proposed Prayer Book which General Convention authorized for trial use during the next three years was always known by that makeshift title—*The Book Annexed*.

When the book appeared, it was favorably received. *The Living Church* threw bouquets: "The Committee give to the Church a wonderful volume considered as a Liturgical contribution, and one drawn up by so many different minds. There must have been great self-sacrifice, great charity, great courtesy as well as great learning to have produced it." Then it added, "Let every delegate resolve that he will consider this whole subject in a broad and liberal spirit."[4]

The endorsement of *The Book Annexed* for testing during the next three years was shepherded through the House of Deputies

by Doctor Huntington, secretary of the Joint Committee and
obviously its strong, wise, knowledgeable proponent. *The Book
Annexed* was ratified with what appeared to be "genuine hearti-
ness," as one clergyman put it, by the almost unanimous vote
of the Convention. And *The Living Church* reported:

Even those who were not entirely pleased with the report and the
Book Annexed cannot help admiring the ability, adroitness, acuteness
and energy with which the Reverend Doctor Huntington carries this
business through the House.[5]

Initially, in one quarter at least, the whole matter was one
of surprising indifference. *The Southern Churchman,* published
in Richmond, Virginia, observed languidly after the adjournment of the 1883 Convention:

Considering the conservatism of General Convention the fact that
there were Prayer Book amendments shows some feel the need (although we do not). If so large a body of earnest churchmen desired
changes, there was no reason why they should not have them, if only
the evils resulting from making changes can be prevented.[6]

But it was not long before voices became critical and shrill.
"The language of new rubrics and prayers is not up to the
standard of the old Book," Maryland's diocesan committee reported, and recommended that *The Book Annexed* not be
adopted without an entire revision. (In contrast, the Marylanders
in the Diocese of Easton had enthusiastically endorsed the Book
several months before.) "The liberty given to individual congregations is . . . tending to destroy the uniformity of our Common
Prayer," wrote one *Living Church* respondent. It is "far below"
the 1549 Book and "even inferior" to the 1790 Book, wrote another. Another complained of the "bewildering quantity of
'or this's.' "[7]

From other quarters came praise and endorsement. "Flexibility
and enrichment," the key words in the rationale for *The Book
Annexed,* "are desirable, especially in large centers of population,"
the Bishop of Chicago told his people.[8] And as though he had
taken all the carping criticism he could stand, the Reverend
F. W. Hilliard wrote *The Living Church*:

What did the Church want, not negatively but positively? She wanted elasticity and enrichment. Now the cry is, "By what you allow to be left out, and by what you permit to be put in, you have well-nigh destroyed the identity of the Prayer Book." It may be asserted with confidence, that not one liberty has been granted by way of omission which was not quite generally demanded before the Committee was appointed, while the new matter introduced ... [was] selected from a mass of material by ... [a committee of very competent people].[9]

In the course of the three years there were many suggestions about details. Here are a few:

● The Ten Commandments have no place in Holy Communion. The Commandments are a "liturgical novelty" in any service save the Catechism.

● The Nicene Creed should be in the first person plural "as it was before Rome tinkered with it."

● In speaking of the proper place of the sermon as after the Gospel, rather than after the Creed as it had been in every Prayer Book beginning with 1549, the Reverend Doctor N. W. Camp of Washington, D.C., observed that the sermon was often called the "postil" in medieval English because it came after the reading of the Scripture—a corruption of *post illa verba.*

● In Morning Prayer *The Book Annexed* gave the *Benedictus es* as an alternate to the *Te Deum.* This was tagged "a new fad of our liturgists ... releasing them from the necessity of committing themselves to the strong sentiments of the *Te Deum* any oftener than need be."

By the end of the three-year trial period the winds of sentiment regarding *The Book Annexed* had shifted almost 180 degrees. "A remarkable change has taken place ... since the time when *The Book Annexed* was adopted with much enthusiasm and with practically unanimity at Philadelphia three years ago," observed *The Churchman* on the eve of the 1886 Convention.[10] Negative feelings ran strong: "Faulty in many details"; "few desirable features"; reconstitute the committee "to include liturgical experts"; "the main idea of corporate worship Godward has been more or less subordinated to the manward purpose of supplying popular needs"; so ran the comments in *The Living*

Church during the month of July, three months before the Convention.

The 1886 Convention was conservative, reflecting the Church's sober second thoughts about *The Book Annexed*. Some of the proposal⸀ of the 1883 Convention were adopted; others were rejected, although ⸒dditional proposals were made. The Convention reconsidered some of the latter, and the remainder were referred to a newly-constituted Joint Committee which was to report to the 1889 Convention.

As the time for the 1889 Convention approached and the Joint Committee's report was circulated to the deputies and bishops, voices of protest were again heard. "The committee has gone beyond its commission." "The report contains new proposals not hitherto considered." Bishop Paret of Maryland took a dim view of the whole matter:

I am satisfied that a substantial majority of the clergy never desired revision, and that the overwhelming majority of the lay people regret that a line or a word was touched. Their quiet unwillingness has been lost in the restless eagerness of a minority hungry for change.[11]

He seemed to overlook the fact that the Joint Committee was doing its work at the behest of General Convention, and that General Convention, representing the whole Church, had the authority to accept or reject any or all of the committee's recommendations.

Liturgical revision took precedence over all else at the 1889 Convention. There was a long debate on whether to pass only what had been passed in 1886 and thus end the revision process. This was defeated and the recommendations of the new 1886 committee were incorporated with but few dissenting votes. The mood was "This is final." "The whole Church will rejoice to hear that revision is over," wrote the editor of *The Churchman* shortly after the Convention adjourned (November 2, 1889). It remained only for the 1892 Convention to put the official capstone on the revision process which had been going on, sometimes agonizingly, since 1880.

People have deep feelings about the Prayer Book and it is easy for them to erupt in bitter polemic exaggeration. This was sometimes true in the press during the years of revision. But the mood was commendably different in the Houses of General

Convention in 1889. Here is a post-Convention description of what it was like:

The most earnest discussions have been free from partisan asperity, and while the widest differences of opinion have been freely and energetically maintained, the most perfect personal courtesy and every token of sincere respect have been exhibited. The brotherly tolerance which has been conspicuous in the Church for many years seems to have grown in brotherly appreciation which enables men, however they differ in opinion, not only to respect each other's rights, but to enter appreciatively into each other's reasons. It might be too much to say that there is a manifest reaction from all extreme views; but it is not too much to say that in the Convention just closed extreme opinions were neither sharply nor offensively defined, and that a spirit of commendable moderation was at all times apparent.[12]

The 1892 Convention was businesslike and determined that nothing would be permitted to set aside or delay the completion of Prayer Book revision. All resolutions which would have blocked the immediate completion of the task were voted down. The task was completed by noon, October 11, 1892. The Church had a new Book of Common Prayer.

Here are the principal ways in which the 1892 Book differs from its predecessor of a hundred years before:

● The whole text of the *Benedictus* is restored.

● Permission to omit the descent-into-hell clause is withdrawn.

● The *Magnificat* and *Nunc dimittis* are restored.

● An anthem is permitted in Evening Prayer after the Third Collect.

● There are additions to the Prayers and Thanksgivings.

● Material from the 1662 Commination is used in "A Penitential Office for Ash Wednesday."

● The Decalogue may be omitted at times.

● The Nicene Creed is printed in Holy Communion and must be used on the five great festivals.

● A hymn is no longer required after the Prayer of Consecration.

● The Book of Acts reading (8:14–17) is added to the Confirmation Service.

● A hymn, the Creed, and prayers may be inserted after the Lesson in the Burial Service.

It was a very conservative revision of the Book, especially considering the years of discussion and the number of proposed changes. Marion Hatchett comments that "almost every peculiarity of the 1790 Book was retained."

Unquestionably, the primary force behind the movement for revision was Doctor William Reed Huntington. It was his resolution which had set the process in motion back in 1880. He was secretary of the first Joint Committee on Revision which served until 1886 and was the recognized floor leader in the debates on the subject in all five Conventions, 1880–1892. Huntington was respected and admired by his colleagues, not only for his ability but also for his affability and kind consideration of everyone. *The Churchman* of October 22, 1892, spoke of him as a man of "consummate tact ... so conciliatory that his very opponents cannot help wishing they could agree with him, even when they are compelled to differ." Among other leaders of the House of Deputies at the 1892 Convention who, along with Huntington, were responsible for the smooth and successful passage of the Book, were Doctor Samuel Hart of Connecticut, who represented the Joint Committee, and Doctor Dix of New York, President of the House.

That same Convention adopted a new *Hymnal. The Hymnal, Revised and Enlarged with Music*, contained 679 hymns. This was quite an advance over what had been authorized for use formerly. Back in 1786, fifty-one hymns and eight pages of tunes had been added at the end of the Proposed Prayer Book of that year. The 1789 Book reduced that number to twenty-seven and no tunes were given. The General Convention of 1826 adopted a *Hymnal* of 212 texts which was known as the "Prayer Book Collection" because Convention ordered that it be bound in with the Prayer Book. Two years later the Rev. Jonathan Mayhew Wainwright, rector of Grace Church, New York, published a tune-book. The tunes were assigned to the texts by indexes. The first *Hymnal* of respectable proportions was authorized by the Convention of 1871. It contained 520 hymns and was bound separately from the Prayer Book. In 1886 another revision was launched which resulted in the *Hymnal* adopted by the 1892 General Convention.[13]

It is hard for us to grasp the extent to which the worship of the Episcopal Church had changed between the time when the first American Prayer Book passed the General Convention of 1789 and the time when its successor was adopted at the 1892 Convention. Marion Hatchett helps us realize how great that change was:

In architecture, Episcopal Churches had moved from Georgian (or meetinghouse Colonial), to Hopkins' precursor of Gothic, to Upjohn (and carpenter's Gothic), to Richardson (and shingled Romanesque), almost to Cram. In music, it had moved from Metrical Psalms and the soberest of hymns, to Anglican chant and even some Gregorian chant, Romantic and Victorian hymnology, and the Tucker Hymnal. The pipe or reed organ had ousted the village instrumentalists, and the quartet or surpliced choir (now sitting up front) had ousted the parish clerk. In ceremonial, the Altar had replaced the Holy Table; Eucharistic vestments had in many places replaced the surplice, and the use of the gown was almost gone; superfrontals (changed according to the Roman color sequence) had replaced the Laudian frontal. At the revision of the Prayer Book [1789], the Signation in the Baptismal rite had been optional; by the time the Prayer Book was revised, multitudinous crossings were often to be seen in the Eucharistic Prayer. In 1790 a candle or cross would hardly have been tolerated on any Holy Table; by 1892 they were found on almost all Altars.[14]

Such were the changes in emphasis and fashion in that hundred years. The revision of 1892, with its flexibility and enrichment, was intended to be the book of the new day.

CHAPTER VIII

The Book of 1928

The members of the Convention of 1892 were no doubt certain they were providing a Book of Common Prayer which would serve the Church for a long time to come, as its predecessor had done. But their vision was upset by the unrubrical visions of a thirty-year-old engineer in Detroit named Henry Ford, who had just started his automobile manufacturing company, and a couple of young bicycle-making brothers named Wright, who at Kitty Hawk, North Carolina, flew a contraption 120 feet. The year was 1903, and the world would never again be as it had been in 1892. The ripple effect touched all of life.

So it is not surprising that a decade later memorials were presented to the General Convention of 1913 by the Dioceses of California and Arizona asking that a Joint Commission be appointed to consider revising and enriching the Prayer Book. Their spokesman was the Reverend Edward L. Parsons, and his reasoning was as unthreatening and tentative as the touch-down of a butterfly: "There are several parts of the Prayer Book which might be revised and enriched whereby it would be better adapted for present use."[1]

The Joint Commission was appointed and instructed to report to the next General Convention. Three years later, Archduke Ferdinand of Austria had been assassinated, and Europe was in flames when the General Convention met at St. Louis. The preoccupation of American churchmen thus was not entirely ecclesiastical, even in St. Louis. "The subject of revision should not be entered upon at this time," wrote Doctor L. Bradford Price in the columns of *The Churchman*.[2]

But there were others who thought it should not only be entered upon, but that its scope should be considerably widened. Thirty-nine clergymen memorialized the General Convention of

1916, arguing that revision should be more thorough and comprehensive than had been contemplated by the last General Convention—greater emphasis on the Church missionary vocation and its social responsibilities, less emphasis on the depravity of men ("miserable sinners," "conceived and born in sin," etc.), and, recognizing the principle of unity with variety, greater latitude in worship. This was going to be something more than what had been called "the infinitesimal revision of the early 90's."

Parsons, "a most persuasive and unruffled spokesman," presented the Commission's recommendations in twenty-three resolutions. Some of them passed, but there was much unfinished business for the Commission to work on before the next General Convention. The more significant liturgical accomplishment of the 1916 Convention was the adoption of a new *Hymnal. The Churchman*, a publication which always took a great interest in the church's music, called it one of "an exceptional kind . . . a visible demonstration of the liberality of the Convention to new devotional demands." It contained 559 hymns: 126 new ones added, 200 old ones dropped. Final action to make it official was to be taken in 1919.[3]

The time between the Conventions of 1916 and 1919 was reckoned by everybody in terms of world events—the submarine blockade, President Wilson leading the way to make the world safe for democracy, the Armistice, the Treaty of Versailles, the League of Nations. Again in 1919 the Church found it difficult to give Prayer Book revision center stage. The Church press in the months preceding the Convention in Detroit repeatedly argued that this was no time for the Church to tinker with words and phrases "while human society throughout the world is being upturned from its very foundation." In August the report of the Joint Commission was available, and there were persistent voices urging that it be set aside until 1922.

But there were others who cleaned their spectacles and gave that report serious attention. The Reverend Walker Gwynne wrote in *The Southern Churchman*, "The Report as a whole . . . shows not only great and painstaking thought, but it is to be commended for its conservative as well as its progressive character in recognizing . . . the needs of the new day." But Doctor Randolph McKim, who analyzed the Report in a series of articles in that same Richmond, Virginia, periodical, disagreed and

took violent exception to "this so-called 'Revision.' Every service
is changed—some so radically as to be hardly recognized. . . .
There is a vital change in our doctrinal position." He damned
the whole Report with the comment, "It is more in harmony
with the fifteenth century than the twentieth. To a large extent
it has been written with a pen dipped in sacerdotalism." And
at the Convention another southerner hinted ominously of schism.
"The Church is at the parting of the ways," the Reverend
James M. Owens of Louisiana was reported as saying.[4]

The 1919 Convention was a disappointment. Hardly a tenth
of the Commission's recommendations had been acted upon in
1916. Some of these revisions passed a second reading—Morning
Prayer, Evening Prayer, parts of Prayers and Thanksgivings,
and The Psalter—but little new material was agreed upon. And
there were many frustrations. For example, the Burial Office
had passed both Houses of Convention in 1916, but due to a
technical error in the Secretary's Office of the House of Bishops
it was thrown out. In 1919 the Deputies again passed it, but
the Bishops did not get to it. So it would all have to be done
again in 1922. No wonder Parsons, the spokesman of the Commission, called the Convention's work "disappointing"; however,
he added, "when one remembers how widespread was the
sentiment in favor of deferring all consideration whatever of
revision, what was accomplished must be viewed with gratitude."[5]

Perhaps the most interesting comment on Prayer Book revision
was that of the Reverend Thomas L. Cole in *The Churchman*
a month before the 1919 Convention. He urged that the General
Convention authorize a "trying out" of the Commission's proposed changes in the services, and that on a basis of the results,
the final report should be adopted by General Convention "as
a whole, without amendment or discussion of detail." He also
said that those responsible should include women.[6] Fifty years
later the Church followed his advice almost to the letter.

A new resolution to get the job done seemed to pervade the
Church as the 1922 General Convention approached. The Commission's Report in 1916 had broken new ground and helped
the Church realize how much revision was needed. That report
was received with commendation. But before 1919, conservative
forces assisted by postwar reaction slowed the process. The
Commission's Report of that year was not as popular as its

predecessor and was picked at dishearteningly. Now the third Report of the Commission was being thoroughly studied more with an eye to workability than to carping.

The tone of the Convention was set by the calm wisdom of Bishop Edwin S. Lines, who in his sermon at the opening of the Convention put Prayer Book revision in its proper setting and perspective:

The Prayer Book, which remains substantially as nearly four centuries ago when hardly anyone had books and few could read and life for the majority of people was narrow and hard, needs many changes. It is a new age, and its new hopes and duties must find expression in the services of the Church. The former Revision [1892] was closed in a spirit of reaction, much that we needed was not obtained. Despite the insistent demand to bring Revision to an end, and the anxieties of conservative people, always to be respected, we should, with patience, give suitable time to this work. The world moves so fast that something in the way of Revision may be required in every generation. If the Church does not make a reasonable Revision to meet these new needs there will be danger of individual revisions which will weaken the great tradition of common worship.[7]

There was section by section, service by service, line by line detailed consideration of Baptism, Matrimony, Burial, the Ordinal, and the Churching of Women. The vote was generally close with much spirited discussion. Cautious voices like Bishop Bratton of Mississippi reminded those who might have been carried away by the new and different, "Our people are devoted to the Prayer Book as it is. We should have good reason for any changes which we make." Some even desired to table the whole matter, and octogenarian Bishop Tuttle, who had been Presiding Bishop for nearly twenty years, was quoted in the press as saying "that the industrial situation, the rights of women, and the way to obtain world peace were more important than questions concerning forms and ceremonies."[8]

Nevertheless, the 1922 Convention made encouraging progress even though Revision was not completed, and the House of Deputies authorized the publication of a pamphlet listing the alterations in the Book of Common Prayer which had been finally adopted by the Conventions of 1919 and 1922, and a second list of those proposed alterations passed by the present Convention which were to be ratified. Finally, General Convention instructed the Joint Commission not to present to the 1925 Convention any new proposals beyond those in their report to the present Convention. Even the least optimistic could begin to see light at the end of the tunnel.

There was little general reaction to the Convention's efforts toward Prayer Book revision. Perhaps the reassurance of Bishop Johnson, editor of *The Witness,* was felt even by those who did not read his words:

The General Convention finished its revision of the Prayer Book so far as Morning and Evening Prayer is concerned . . . the slight changes in these offices ought to reassure members of the Church that no revision of other offices . . . will be any more far reaching or drastic than in the final revision already accomplished.[9]

One of the positive effects of the 1922 Convention had to do with churchmanship. Among the revision proposals was one to include the *Benedictus Qui Venit* ("Blessed is he that cometh in the name of the Lord") after the *Sanctus* for optional use. The High Churchmen wanted thus to make official what was a general practice among them. The Low Churchmen strongly objected to its inclusion since it was taken from the Roman Missal. On theological grounds, the Joint Commission did not recommend its inclusion. Although there were some strong churchmanship feelings expressed, the overall effect was of a different sort. In looking back one member of the Convention observed:

Everyone remarks how the old partisan lines have been erased. The contentious party-man is out of fashion. Inclusiveness for all sincere Christians is the aim and ideal. . . . The fearful folk who distrust their brethren of other interpretations of the faith found themselves in a significant minority.[10]

A generation later, in the heyday of the Christian education revival of the 1950s, this description by the Reverend Phillip E. Osgood really became generally true.

In the late summer of 1925, the Joint Commission issued their fourth report in advance of the meeting of the General Convention. It was in two parts: a few obvious corrections of the services finally passed in 1922 and new material to be considered—Saints' Days, some new Collects, Epistles, and Gospels, and a few Lectionary changes. The explanation in the Church press of Bishop Slattery, a member of the Joint Commission, sounds as if he were addressing himself to the revision of fifty years later:

We are trying to avoid vain repetitions, the use of archaic words or phrases which, to the ordinary layman, mean either nothing or something untrue and such length of prayer or praise in any one part of any service that the mind becomes numb and the worship of the heart ceases.... Everyone ought to ask if he would not be a more collected worshipper if the Prayer of Consecration in the Holy Communion were much shorter than it is.

Later, in his explanation of the permissive options in Morning Prayer, he set a standard of Prayer Book worship which every parishioner wishes were tattooed on his rector's determination:

The rector is bound, if he does his duty, to use his freedom with careful preparation. He may unify the service, by his choice of Psalm, prayers and hymns, to make these, with the Lessons and sermon, one massive expression of Christian truth and devotion.[11]

As the Convention opened, the editor of *The Churchman* warned the deputies against the temptation which besets all churchmen in their love of the Prayer Book:

The chief task of the Convention in this matter [of Revision] is not to preserve for our delectation a sacred literary monument, but to provide prayers which any intelligent Christian can say with sincerity. And not to desire this sincerity, to remain content with the present lack of coordination between religion and life, is nothing short of a sin.[12]

There was a feeling among many in the Church that the time was now. "We have now reached the most critical stage of the entire revision. Because there was decided progress in 1922, the ratification of that progress must be made in 1925, or it fails ... there would be little incentive to proceed to consider the material that has not yet been taken up. The revision movement would be a failure." And as though the work of the Convention were a foregone conclusion, the editor of *The Living Church* threw the usual closing-ritual bouquet of accolades to the Commission:

It remains for us to compliment the Joint Commission and its members upon their work during these twelve years since its first appointment. There have been many changes in personnel. . . . Through it all there has been constant unswerving attention both to principles and to details. . . . We doubt whether any group of learned men, differing among themselves in details of Churchmanship as these gentlemen inevitably do, have ever produced work so devoid of partisanship throughout as this Joint Commission has done. It will be difficult for the Commission to present its recommendations in the House of Deputies at the coming Convention as lucidly, as delicately, and as gracefully as the task has been performed in past years, first by Doctor Parsons and then by Doctor Slattery.[13]*

The frustrations of previous Conventions had tested the stamina and patience of proponents of revision. Now the delegates to the Convention of 1925 sensed that success was within grasping distance. They were not going to allow anything to prevent action which would make final revision certain in 1928. Everyone was swept along—or nearly everyone. Some wanted to drop the whole thing and return to the 1892 Book. This of course was impossible even if desirable, since revision of large sections of the Prayer Book had passed the Conventions of 1919 and 1922, and were now part of whatever official book. Others, while not advocating abortion, took a dim view of much that had been done. Bishop A. C. A. Hall of Vermont was one of these. "The new Office for Burial of a Child would make us a laughingstock in Catholic Christendom." "The Baptismal Service generally is in almost hopeless confusion." As for some of the proposed Collects, he considered them "by no means an improvement." His conclusion was that while all must be anxious for the final settlement of the business of revision in 1928, the Convention should not stampede into hasty endorsements of the Commission's recommendations.[14]

There were also some last minute pleas for still further change. This delightful letter from the Reverend Henry M. Saville of East Providence, Rhode Island, is an example. It is hoped that the world has not moved so fast that we find it impossible to recapture his sense of awe:

I hope it is not too late [the Convention was to convene in four days] to ask the Prayer Book Revisers to add in the Litany to the petition,

---

*By then both had been elected bishops.

"All who travel by land or by water"—"or by air." My greatest feat, when in Europe this past summer, was to fly in an airplane from Paris to London, at ninety miles an hour for two and a half hours, at 1000 feet above the land and water, in the late afternoon of a perfect day! It was the most marvelous experience of my life and a wonderful trip. The prayers of my friends I am sure helped to make the trip so fine and safe, for the risk is great. Such passenger service in Europe is common today. It is bound to come to be so too in this country. May this startling fact be recognized at once in our Litany.[15]

Later that month both Houses of the General Convention voted to add "or by air" to The Litany petition.

The Convention of 1925 set resolutely to work in the shirt-sleeve weather of New Orleans and plodded, dutiful and dripping, through the roll calls necessary to ratify the changes and amendments to Morning and Evening Prayer, Prayers and Thanksgivings, Holy Communion, Collects, Epistles and Gospels, Confirmation, Matrimony, and Burial which had passed the 1922 Convention. Observers noted that there were differences of opinion but that all passed "by safe majorities, and without a ripple of partisanship or a hasty word spoken. The temper and spirit of the Convention are admirable."[16] That Convention had every intention to make official in 1928 the work of revision which had been its center stage concern since 1916.

And that is the way it happened three years later in Washington, D.C.

When the Bishops and Deputies gathered on the grounds of the Washington Cathedral for the opening service of the 1928 General Convention, they knew, as their host, Bishop James Freeman put it, that their "most important work" was "the consummation of Prayer Book revision." Nine days later, Friday, October 19, 1928, Doctor John W. Suter, secretary of the Prayer Book Revision Commission, presented a resolution in the House of Deputies declaring that the revision of 1928 was accepted as the text of the Book of Common Prayer.

Here are the ways in which this third American Prayer Book differs from its 1892 predecessor:

● The new Lectionary. To use Bishop Slattery's words, "It contains the most arresting passages in the Old and New Testament."

● Morning and Evening Prayer. A new rubric makes it possible to omit the General Confession and Absolution; Invitatory Antiphons are added before the *Venite*; the Minister has discretion in the Psalm(s) used; the *Te Deum* is printed in three sections, and a shorter canticle, *Benedictus es, Domine*, may be used in its stead; there is an alternate and more appropriate Prayer for the President, "suitable for the age which believes high office to be not a privilege but a responsibility"; the Prayer for the President is no longer obligatory in Morning Prayer; there is a wider choice of prayers after the Third Collect; one Lesson is permissible in Evening Prayer.

●Prayers and Thanksgivings. They have been mercifully edited and are shorter and less wordy; they cover almost twice as many subjects; the prayer "For Malefactors after Condemnation" is dropped.

● Collects, Epistles, and Gospels. They have been placed after Holy Communion and archaic phrases have been changed; there are many new Sunday Propers and there are additional Propers for A Saint's Day, the Dedication of a Church, the Ember Days, the Rogation Days, Independence Day (for the first time), Thanksgiving Day, At a Marriage, and At the Burial of the Dead.

● Holy Communion. The Commandments must be said at least "one Sunday in each month" rather than "once on each Sunday." The word "militant" has been dropped from the Prayer for the Whole State and the words, "grant them continual growth in thy love and service," have been added to the petition for the departed. In the rubric before the Prayer of Consecration, "Table" has been changed to "Holy Table." The Lord's Prayer has been added as the conclusion of the Prayer of Consecration and is followed by the Prayer of Humble Access. This latter prayer came at this point in the service in 1549. In 1552 it was moved to a position between the *Sanctus* and the Prayer of Consecration, where it remained up until this time.

● Baptism. The three different services which the Prayer Book has provided since 1662 are telescoped into one. There is more emphasis on the Resurrection and less on original sin. Alternate Gospel readings and a closing Benediction have been added.

● Offices of Instruction. The Catechism has been put in the back of the book, and new Offices of Instruction have been added based on it and with new questions regarding the Church, Confirmation, and the Ministry.

● Confirmation. The old Exhortation has been omitted and there is an additional question to the candidates.

● Matrimony. The blessing of the ring, prayers for children, and that the couple "love, honour, and cherish each other" have been added; the vows are identical; the word "obey" has been dropped from the woman's vow. In the heated debate in the House of Deputies six years earlier, Doctor (later Bishop) George Craig Stewart opposed this change: "To eliminate the word 'obey' from the marriage ritual is a concession to an unpleasant, unwomanly femininity and flapperism."

● Visitation of the Sick. It is an entirely new Office; there is also provision for anointing or the Laying on of Hands.

● Burial. There are additional Psalms and Lessons, alternate sentences at the grave, and "The God of peace" instead of The Grace.

● Services to be used at Sea and for the Visitation of Prisoners are omitted.

● The Psalter. Much sixteenth-century wording is retained, but wrong translations are corrected and the opportunity is given to omit imprecatory verses of certain Psalms.

● Ordination. A special Litany has been added and the questions to Deacons revised.

● Family Prayer. A shorter form is added as well as many additional prayers.

● Articles of Religion. Their inclusion within the covers of the Book has special significance. In 1925 the Convention voted to omit them, but this was obviously very upsetting to a large number, particularly of southern Low Churchmen. So in 1928

by a unanimous vote the Convention reversed itself and left
them in. Doctor Walter C. Whittaker, in commenting on the
Convention, called this action "the salient feature in legislation"
and went on to add, "This action declared to the world that
after all, the different schools within the Church are putting the
cause of Christ above all their party differences."[17]

One of the people deeply involved in the whole revision process was Bishop Charles Slattery. He was a member of the
Joint Commission and for a time the presenter of the Commission's Report to the House of Deputies. Later he was among
its strong proponents in the House of Bishops. His summation
of the 1928 Book was that

Baptism is lifted into the expression of God's love for His children;
the marriage service makes the woman equal to the man in privilege
and responsibility; the burial service substitutes New Testament trust
for Old Testament fear; aspirations of our time for social justice,
good government, and world brotherhood are recognized; services
may be made shorter, and with hymns and sermon, may have a new
force and a new unity. In a word, without ceasing to be the book of
the ages, the Prayer Book becomes also the book of this generation.[18]

Perhaps that which makes this revision of the Prayer Book
unique is the sense of history and the attitude toward their
work both of the Joint Commission and of the Convention.
Most previous revisions had a long life—1559 to 1662, 1662 to
1790, 1790 to 1892—but the 1892 Book had been in use only
twenty-one years when the Joint Commission was appointed
and machinery was set in motion which resulted in the 1928
Book. The world would never again be the leisurely place it
had been, nor the Prayer Book the bulwark of unchanging
stability decade after decade. Moreover, the Anglican Churches
of Scotland, Ireland, Canada, and South Africa had all been
revising their Prayer Books while successive General Conventions were wrestling with the American Book. They had insights
we Americans could not ignore. Also, there were increasing
signs of inter-Church cooperation and liturgical appreciation
which extended across denominational lines. These factors, plus
the giant strides new biblical research was making, all con-

tributed to the conviction that "the book of this generation" would hardly speak to the needs and aspirations of the new day beyond. The Church would need a continuing commission which would be alive to the work of liturgical expression in other Churches as well as in other Anglican Churches, and would stay close to the new discoveries and insights in biblical research. Only thus would the Prayer Book of tomorrow be the adequate expression of the praying people of tomorrow.

The 1922 Convention had said to the Joint Commission, "No more new recommendations beyond this point." But the Commision had additional liturgical insights which the experience of their years of work had not yet brought into sharp focus. So its final report in 1928 stated:

The work of revision is not perfect. No human undertaking is. Every member of the Commission has in mind some further item of change which he would like to see incorporated; but, taking the work as a whole, the Commission believes that much has been accomplished, and that the revision will be welcomed by the people as a genuine help in the advancing life and work of the Church.[19]

General Convention accepted their work in that spirit and before adjourning created a Standing Liturgical Commission of eight Bishops, eight Priests, and eight laymen to which would be referred

for preservation and study, all matters relating to the Book of Common Prayer, with the idea of developing and conserving for some possible future use the Liturgical experience and scholarship of the Church.[20]

No previous General Convention had taken this kind of long, constructive view of its freshly-completed revision. The Convention saw the wisdom of Bishop Lines' words of six years earlier, "The world moves so fast that something in the way of Revision may be required in every generation."

For the twelve years since the 1916 General Convention, because of the recommended changes in the Prayer Book which were being considered and voted upon by successive General Conventions, the tendency throughout the Church was to be quite casual about observing the rubrics in the 1892 Book. Various changes were being experimented with, unofficially for the most part, thus helping churchmen at the grassroots make up their minds about what was being proposed. All this was only natural. But now there was a new, official Book of Common Prayer. The day of rubrical laxity was past. The House of Bishops addressed themselves to this in their Pastoral Letter to all of the clergy:

There is need in the Church as in the State to sound a call to loyalty. Your Bishops, assembled in triennial session, make an appeal for a loyal recognition of our common obligation to render generous obedience in observing in their integrity the provisions of our enriched Book of Common Prayer. . . . Such loyalty does not, of course, preclude as occasions may require, special services as provided for in the rubrics of the Prayer Book or authorized by the Bishops; but it does demand of the authorized Ministers of the Church obedience to the rubrical directions of its authorized book of worship, as at all times binding upon priest and people. These rubrics and the various offices of the Book are the solemn expression of the mind of the Church. . . . The liberty of experimental usage allowed during the period of revision should now cease.[21]

The "enriched Book of Common Prayer" came off the press in the fall of 1929, and, according to a resolution of the House of Bishops, became the only authorized Book of Common Prayer as soon as it was "available for use." The Church Hymnal Corporation provided "a beautifully printed and bound edition" for 25 cents and Morehouse Publishing Company advertised "genuine Morocco bound Prayer Books" for $2.00.

While reactions to the revised Book ran the whole gamut, the traditionally High Church parts of the country were generally more favorable, while the traditionally Low Church parts of the country read Anglo-Catholic and even Roman encroachment into the non-controversial changes. "The new Prayer Book is beautiful. Nothing has been lost through the elisions but much gained through the additions." "Far superior to the old in many ways . . . so few flaws. . . ." *The Witness* considered it "conservative," saying that it represented "the united sentiment of the rank and file of the Episcopal Church."

The clergy of the Diocese of Chicago liked it: "a real step forward on the part of the Church." But a letter to the *Southern Churchman* just before the 1928 Convention convened decried the numerous prayers for the departed which for the author conjured up the specter of Purgatory; changes in the sequence of Holy Communion which he considered "Anglo-Catholic influence"; propers for a wedding and a burial, which were a step toward Romish nuptial and requiem masses. He concluded, "The more the Prayer Book is 'enriched' the poorer it becomes in evangelical religion, in Scriptural and Apostolic Christianity." Week after week following the 1928 Convention, there were critical letters in the church press pointing out the Book's flaws, errors, and inconsistencies. Finally when he could stand no more, A. H. Russell scored the nit-pickers with "It really does seem very weak and foolish to pick up the book to scan for faults and criticism."[22]

Perhaps the most widespread criticism of the Book centered on the Introduction to the Lord's Prayer at the end of the Prayer of Consecration. The 1925 Convention agreed to the words, "And now, as our Saviour Christ hath taught us, let us say." The Joint Commission, using its authority to make editorial changes, revised that preface to read "we are bold to say," so that the words continued to be addressed to the Father, thus making the Lord's Prayer an integral part of the Prayer of Consecration. This latter wording had come from the Scottish Service of 1764 via Seabury's Notebook, and earlier from the Prayer Book of 1549. But when it turned up in 1928 the outcry was loud and widespread. (Here we cross the line from research to memory. The father of the author had one loudly-expressed criticism of the new Book—his snorting contempt for that bit of obvious Anglo-Catholic coloration, "we are *bold* to say." Unknowingly he reenacted in tone and sentiment the spit-out reaction of a Scottish Puritan divine centuries before regarding "that naughty preface." But he was not the only objector. Other priests have similar recollections of the reactions of their fathers who were clergymen in widely different parts of the country.) Just how many felt as strongly as did the Reverend Charles C. Durkee of Elkridge, Maryland, who considered that preface "the most serious indeed the most shocking blot in the new book," is not known.

A significant comment on the new Book came from Bishop Hall of Vermont. In 1925 he had been scathingly antagonistic toward the Book. The services he had criticized severely became a part of the finally-approved Book. In 1929 he publicly declared his loyal adherence to the newly-official Book of Common Prayer:

The Book is not perfect. Some of us may regret this or that change, and others would have preferred further changes. But it is the Standard Book, deliberately adopted according to the prescribed method of the national Church. Individual preference should be subordinated to a loyal and honest conformity to the prescribed form.[23]

The Episcopal Church is strong and its Book of Common Prayer is the treasured liturgical touchstone of Episcopalians and non-Episcopalians alike, in part at least because of this kind of loyal devotion to its formularies.

The wise and honest observation of E. Clowes Chorley, Historiographer of the Episcopal Church, put into words the feelings of many of his fellow clergy and at the same time led them into the new day:

We cannot lay aside the old Book without a pang of regret. It had become endeared to us by thirty-seven years of use. But that regret will be momentary. With all its defects—and there are such—the new Prayer Book is immeasurably superior to the old.[24]

He was right. Others discovered the truth of his words, and in a remarkably short time after the Book came officially into use it was accepted, used without murmuring, and, very shortly, loved.

CHAPTER IX

The Proposed Book of 1976

The world of 1928 is almost inconceivably remote from the world of 1976, when General Convention adopted the Draft Proposed Book as the Proposed Book of Common Prayer.

The world of 1928 is so different that we can hardly imagine what it was like. Since that time, communication has added television and the use of satellites; sound movies have become an everyday medium of entertainment; the plastic age has transformed the manufacturing world; jet plane travel is the standard; and men have walked on the moon. In ecclesiastical circles life has moved with a similar rapidity. The discovery of the Dead Sea Scrolls has ushered in a new day of biblical research. Roman Catholic scholars and later Protestant scholars have been pushing back beyond the Middle Ages and coming to the conclusion that the liturgical expressions through which the early Church presented the Christian faith communicate more significantly to twentieth-century worshippers than do medieval forms. And as the roots of worship become more ancient, its ecumenical potential becomes greater. Doors between Christian Churches have begun to open more widely than had been thought possible.

In the Church of England, A. G. Hebert was stretching liturgical thinking with his books *Liturgy and Society* (1935) and *The Parish Communion* of which he was the editor in 1937. The result was that the almost-universal Sunday schedule of Holy Communion at 8:00 and Morning Prayer at 11:00 began to shift toward the more ancient pattern of a parish communion at 9:00 in which the laity actively participated—joining in prayers formerly said by the priest alone, reading the Epistle, making responses to the various petitions in the Prayer for the Church, bringing up the elements at the Offertory, and assisting with the chalice.[1] These revolutionary ideas and prac-

84

tices—the liturgical movement, it was called—began finding their way into the thinking of the American Church, thanks to the efforts of such scholars as William P. Ladd, Theodore O. Wedel, Massey H. Shepherd, Jr., and others.

The push toward consideration of revision was the result of the happenstance concert of significant forces: the liturgical movement, the ecumenical movement with its roots in a twentieth-century understanding of mission, and the revival of biblical theology. So it is not surprising that in 1950 the Standing Liturgical Commission began a detailed review of the 1928 Book. This resulted in the publication of the first wave of Prayer Book Studies (Nos. 1–16). These studies recommended changes, but they were hardly more than timid liturgical manicures of services in the 1928 Book—the pattern of change followed in 1892 and 1928. But the Bishops of the Anglican Communion of the 1958 Lambeth Conference were thinking in more drastic terms, and the subsequent Anglican Congress of 1963 set forth ecumenically broad liturgical guidelines which were based on Early Church practice. The Church of South India and the Church of India, Pakistan, Burma, and Ceylon had already moved in that direction and, before the General Convention met in 1964, a milestone Liturgy for Africa had come out.

The liturgical movement was like an avalanche sweeping down the mountainside of modern Christendom. To stand aside from it would have been to step onto a crag and let it pass, only then to realize that our Church was an isolated, left-behind bit of Christendom, separated from the world of the present and its needs, impotent and alone. Such timidity was not for a moment considered. The General Convention of 1964 recognized "a growing desire in various parts of the Church for revision," saying that "the time seems right to many in the Church to undertake a revision of the Book of Common Prayer." The Standing Liturgical Commission was instructed "to propose to the next General Convention . . . a plan" for trial use of a proposed revision "with a special view to making the language and the forms of the services more relevant to the circumstances of the Church's present ministry and life."[2] The vote was almost unanimous. Bishop Chilton Powell was the recently-appointed chairman of the commission, and Charles M. Guilbert, who had succeeded John W. Suter, Jr., as Custodian of the Book of Common Prayer in 1962, was secretary.

The commission's report to the 1967 General Convention summarized the pressures toward Prayer Book revision which should not be ignored:

1. The spiritual and pastoral needs of the present are not being met by the present Book.

2. The rubrics in the 1928 Book are frequently inconsistent and misleading. Reconciling the rubrics was one of the unfinished tasks of the last revision.

3. The growing desire to use other translations of the Bible brings into sharp focus the fact that the meanings of many prayers are not well understood by large numbers of people, especially the young.

4. In recent decades the history, principles, and significance of worship have been the objects of deep and widespread study by scholars of a wide variety of Christian Churches. As a result, other parts of the Anglican Communion and other major Christian bodies—Protestant and Catholic—have revised liturgies in this decade. In the Eucharist especially there is increasing ecumenical agreement about the pattern and form of the service. This agreement is consistent with both the doctrines and the traditions this Church has always maintained. Episcopalians naturally do not wish to fall into the background, since the successive revisions of the Book of Common Prayer have set the highest standard of Christian worship in the English-speaking world.

The plan for trial use which the previous Convention had directed the Liturgical Commission to formulate was adopted. It recognized the fact that Prayer Book revision is "a difficult and delicate process, calling for spiritual depth, theological balance, literary beauty, and pastoral practicality," and that it requires the best knowledge, talent, and experience available throughout the Church. Therefore, the proposed plan was that 200 consultants be selected (actually it was nearly 300 before the work was completed), some of whom serve on Drafting Committees and some of whom are Reader-Consultants. Each Committee has a single service or section of the Prayer Book for which it is responsible to produce a preliminary draft revision. A member of the Standing Liturgical Commission is chairman and liaison with the Commission, which is responsible for assembling the entire proposed revision for presentation to the 1970 Convention. The material thus produced is to be tested in "a public, orderly, and democratic manner in actual services of worship." The resulting comments, criticisms, and suggestions are then to be analyzed and the original material revised. In this way the clergy and laity of the whole Church play a direct part in the development and revision of new liturgical forms.

To begin the process, the Standing Liturgical Commission presented *The Liturgy of the Lord's Supper* for trial use. It had not been casually concocted. The commission reported that it had been tested (both said and sung) for more than a decade in various congregations, and had already gone through eleven editions. It was as a result of this careful preparation that the commission considered the service "worthy of being presented to the Church." In that service the considerations leading to revision were more broadly based than simply on an analysis of that same service in the Prayer Book already in use. One factor was Dom Gregory Dix's *The Shape of the Liturgy* (1945), which argued for the ancient sequence of the Offertory just before the *Sursum Corda* ("Lift Up Your Hearts"), and the Fraction (the breaking of the bread) as a separate act following the Eucharistic Prayer. This sequence, justified by ancient practice and ecumenically recognized, had been recommended by the Anglican Bishops at Lambeth in 1958. A practice which was becoming widespread about this same time and which became associated with the new Liturgy was that of clergy celebrating Communion facing the people. Again ancient custom was infiltrating modern practice. Sometimes this was done by moving the Altar out a bit from the east wall; sometimes it was a nave Altar in front of the chancel steps. "In either case it was possible for the celebrant to face westwards, thus adding a visual association with the Last Supper, and emphasizing that the real celebrant is Christ himself."[3]

The 1967 General Convention authorized *The Liturgy of the Lord's Supper* for trial use for three years. But that General Convention went far beyond merely trying out this one service. It assigned to the Standing Liturgical Commission responsibility for "bringing to completion the process of producing a Draft Revised Book of Common Prayer." The show was on the road.

While feedback was coming in from the use of *The Liturgy of the Lord's Supper,* the Drafting Committees were busy preparing trial revisions of the whole Prayer Book. What the Commission was learning from the grassroots reactions of congregations throughout the Church was of inestimable value. Among the things they learned was that, while there was deep attachment to the traditional language of the Prayer Book, there was also a widespread desire to modernize the language of the Communion Service as had already been done by the Roman Catholics and other Christian Churches. Another trend prominent in the correspondence was the desire for wide latitude to experiment with new forms of eucharistic worship. The conclusion was that no single liturgical structure would serve all needs and that the regularly-used services would have to be in both traditional and contemporary English. Before the three years were over, the Commission sent out a questionnaire asking (among other things), "Do you feel that a revision of the 1928 Liturgy is needed?" and "Do you feel that the Trial Liturgy is on the right track?" The replies were overwhelmingly favorable—89% for the first question, 87% for the second.

Bolstered by this and other encouraging indicators, the Standing Liturgical Commission reported to the 1970 Convention that the trial use procedure authorized by the 1967 Convention and used on *The Liturgy of the Lord's Supper* had been fully vindicated. The Commission recommended its further use. As a result, the 1970 Convention authorized a whole series of rites for trial use during the next three years. They were called *Services for Trial Use* which, because of the Book's green-banana color, shortly became known as the *"Green Book."*

But when the *Green Book* landed in the pews, many communicants hit the ceiling. "Who do 'they' think they are, revising the Lord's Prayer and the Creeds and putting services in disgraceful, modern language? What irreverence!" And they objected to God's being addressed familiarly as "You." One offended churchman wrote indignantly to John Hines, the Presiding Bishop, "If Jesus Christ could just know what they are doing to his Prayer Book, he would turn over in his grave!" The offending translations of Creeds and Lord's Prayer were part of the work of the International Consultation on English Texts.

When the various English-speaking Churches across the world, both Protestant and Catholic, began producing modern language liturgies, there was the prospect of there being a number of versions of commonly-used texts—the Lord's Prayer, the Creeds, and others. Such a circumstance would hinder inter-Church cooperation in a day when the ecumenical tide was rising. Those differences would also be confusing to lay people who ventured beyond the confines of their own church, and, of course, would be a nightmare to church musicians. To avoid this unnecessary dilemma, Roman Catholic scholars took the initiative in calling together their compeers in other Churches to deal with the problem. Thus the International Consultation on English Texts (ICET) came into being in 1969. A similar group—Consultation on Common Texts—had been formed in the United States the previous year at the initiative of the Missouri Synod Lutherans. The ICET included Roman Catholics, Anglicans, Lutherans, Presbyterians, Congregationalists, Methodists and Baptists from all over the English-speaking world—United States, Canada, England, Scotland, Ireland, Wales, Australia, and South Africa. They issued *Prayers We Have in Common* in 1970 and the next year revised and enlarged it. That work includes the Lord's Prayer, the Nicene and Apostles' Creeds, *Gloria in excelsis, Sanctus, Benedictus, Gloria Patri, Sursum Corda, Agnus Dei, Te Deum, Nunc dimittis*, and *Magnificat*. Churches were invited to use these texts on an experimental basis in the new liturgies they were preparing. The Standing Liturgical Commission included those new texts in *Services for Trial Use* in 1970.

During the three years between General Conventions, the *Green Book* was widely used. Some church people missed the point. They assumed, perhaps because *Services for Trial Use* was nicely printed on slick paper rather than on newsprint, that all was fixed and final. They froze into unaccepting opposition and could not believe that the words "trial use" meant what they said: the Commission wanted the services tried, and wanted peoples' reactions. Others thought the Commission desired statistical results, ballots for or against. But thanks to the hard work of many a diocesan liturgical commission, a large part of the Church understood that questionnaires regarding the services were designed to be a convenient instrument of communication between the people of the Church, clergy and lay,

and the Commission. Trial use and the accompanying questionnaires were giving all the members of the Church an opportunity
to share in the process of revision.

The sheer volume of correspondence received by the Commission indicated that the services were having wide exposure
and were receiving searching scrutiny by all kinds of church
people—priests and lay persons of all ages, all types of congregations. Many decried the "loss of beautiful English" and
"watered-down theology"; denounced multiple choices and optional services, and urged that "the 1928 Book be retained without change—forever and ever!" "Why change just for the sake
of change?" or "in order to appeal to the young?" "Why not
comply with the wishes of the people?" Other correspondents
were less upset and negative: "I like the traditional wording
but I also like the flexibility." "Let us preserve the magnificent
Book of Common Prayer except where necessary to clarify meanings of words which have changed throughout the years, or
where the interpretations of original texts has proven to be
false." "I'm in my 85th year and I hope I'll live to be as familiar
with the new system as I am with the old."

What many people found hard to comprehend was that their
reactions were taken seriously. A major portion of the time of
each Drafting Committee was spent in considering the views,
observations, criticisms, and suggestions which reached them.
The office of Leo Malania, the Coordinator of Prayer Book
Revision, was a liturgical Grand Central Station—receiving mail
from the field and channeling it to the appropriate committee
or committees, receiving revised drafts of services and sections
of the Prayer Book and sending them to the Reader-Consultants,
receiving their careful comments and suggestions and forwarding
them to the proper committees. Many dedicated servants of
the Church burned much midnight oil. The reactions to the
Green Book reconfirmed what had been learned from the use
of *The Liturgy of the Lord's Supper*. There was no question
but that the revision of the Prayer Book must meet the desire
to preserve the traditional, more formal language of the 1928
Book; the desire to update the Church's language of worship,
as some other branches of Christendom had done; and the
desire for more varied and flexible forms of worship—more open-
ness, greater spontaneity, more lay participation.

In 1973, the Standing Liturgical Commission furthered the process of trial use with the publication of *Authorized Services,* which reflected insights gained from the Church's reactions to *Services for Trial Use,* just as the latter had reflected feedback from the use of *The Liturgy of the Lord's Supper.* Again there was a flood of correspondence from all over the country.

"*Authorized Services* is a great improvement over the *Green Book.* The Second Order had good style and unity. The words flow easily."

"The Peace is artificial in the middle of the service, but the format and typographic design of *Authorized Services* is outstanding."

"I do not like the Canticles, but very much like 'conceived by the power of the Holy Spirit.'"

"The great positive approach of the new is excellent, but the older order has a beauty of its own—it's comforting to know the familiar and to be at peace with it. But the 'new' is more challenging."

"Holy Baptism is beautiful!"

The General Convention of 1973 instructed the Commission to complete its work and to produce a *Draft Proposed Book of Common Prayer* twelve months before the next Convention.

That deadline was met.

The *Draft Proposed Book* represents nine years of trial use. "No other method," ran the Commission's report which accompanied the Book, "could have resulted in the production of so comprehensive and so rich a book of common worship, bringing together within a single volume so wide a spectrum of traditional and contemporary forms."[4]

That report also pointed out what many American Episcopalians did not realize, namely, that the *Draft Proposed Book* (dubbed *The Blue Book* because of its sky-blue cover) was a significant milestone in the long history of the Book of Common Prayer. It is

the first major revision of an Anglican Prayer Book, incorporating many new liturgical principles, recovering much of the historical tradition common to all Christian churches, and to Anglican churches in particular, and aiming towards the greatest possible comprehensiveness. It is only natural to expect intensive interest on the part of churches that find themselves at different stages of the same process.[5]

Most churchmen did not know that the Anglican Church of Canada had actively shared in the period of trial use and that scholars of the Lutheran, Roman, Presbyterian, and Methodist Churches had cooperated with the Commission. The *Draft Proposed Book* had not been produced in a dark corner but in the center of a sunlit stadium filled with interested liturgical scholars from other branches of English-speaking Christendom.

Because of the pioneering process by which it was produced, and also because of its contents, the Book will continue to influence the worship of the Episcopal Church even if General Convention should reject it. This is merely a statement of fact; the liturgical clock cannot be turned back to 1928. Too many have had their eyes open to new ways of worship, new methods of participation in the liturgical life of the Church, and a discovery of the fullness of the historical tradition of the Church. A major result of the process of which the *Draft Proposed Book* was now a visible symbol was renewed and increasingly-informed interest in the worship of the Church.

The reaction to the appearance of the *Draft Proposed Book* was immediate, voluminous, Church-wide, and overwhelmingly favorable. Here is a minute sampling of what they said:

"As a lay person ... I want to commend the Commission ... I am particularly impressed with the quality of the contemporary language material, and the effort to retain much that is dearly loved by many people in terms of traditional language. . . . Especially to be commended is the theological comprehensiveness, the greatly widened theological perspective of this Book."

"I am aware of how impossible it is to put together a Book of Common Prayer that will totally please everyone. And I am willing to live with some things that go against my literary or theological sense."

"The teaching value of the whole Book is immense."

"Reading it has left me deeply moved and mightily impressed by the scholarship and devotion that you and the other members of the Standing Liturgical Commission have exhibited in authoring this volume. Obviously the Holy Spirit did not remove Himself from guiding, forming, and shaping liturgical endeavor with the completion of the 1928 Book. . . . The fruit of our labor is worthy to take its place alongside its predecessors as the Church's Book of Common Prayer."

"There is a real advance in the language over 1928. The imagery, the richness of color and the frankness of the expressions of piety are much more moving, vivid, and biblical than in earlier versions."

"The *Draft Proposed Book* represents the first American Prayer Book I've seen of a disestablished Church. Before now it's been one rite, one King. Even the 1928 Book is an incarnation of an Oath of Conformity and essentially an antidemocratic reality. To say that there can be several rites (in fact, an infinite number) says that it is all right for there to be more than one kind of Christian."

"Even though I am conservative, and one who generally considers change only if it can be put in one's purse, I felt it my duty to try every liturgical option since 1967. I then took exceptions, editorially and otherwise, to many of the earlier proposals. By fine tooth-combing I can still find fault with the *Draft Proposed Book*. But, for the most part I think the Commission had been very responsive to constructive criticism. I think you have a book which should not only satisfy the liturgical needs of the Church for our own time, but provide a pattern for the future as significant as your illustrious Edwardian, Elizabethan, and American predecessors."

". . . several things in particular—the Burial Rite is magnificent, simple, full of gentle Christian joy, and honest. The forms for Reconciliation of a Penitent, especially the second one, are very moving, also the rite for the Adoption of a Child—lovely. Good taste, quiet understatement, and, I think, solid conviction mark the whole book. It makes me proud to be an Episcopalian again."

"Excellent job. . . . It retains almost all the best of the present book, with great enrichment from ancient and modern sources."

"I do not agree with every change, but on the whole, I believe that the Commission has given us a good Book of Common Prayer, a book which the Church can use for the praying of her prayers and the deepening of her faith; I hope it passes the General Convention."

"It is a magnificent work capturing the best that was in the old and at the same time increasing the dimension of Christian worship. The rubrics calling for an increased participation by laymen are particularly forward looking. That particular action will bring greater meaning to worship for more people as the years go by."

And from England, Canon Joseph Poole, sometime Precentor of Canterbury Cathedral under three Archbishops, wrote: "This book runs to 1,001 pages: there is not a page in it but carries evidence of deep scholarship, of a command of fluent English and of accurate syntax, and of a humane Christian spirituality. A huge mass of material has been so skilfully marshalled, and so elegantly presented in print, that nobody need find the book difficult to use."

The focal point of the opposition to the *Draft Proposed Book* was the Society for the Preservation of the Book of Common Prayer (SPBCP). It billboarded its resistance to liturgical change outside the 1976 Convention Hall in Minneapolis just as it had done three years earlier in Louisville. The Society had begun among a group of professors and clergymen in Tennessee in the Spring of 1971 as congealed opposition to the *Green Book.*

The Church does not want the *Green Book.* . . . The Rev. Dr. Massey Shepherd and his partners in Greenbookery would have us declare our buddy-hood with God. . . . A close reading of the best liturgical scholarship raises many questions concerning the historical reasons for changing the liturgy.

So wrote Professor Walter Sullivan, one of the founders and for a time president of the Society.[6] .

Their distaste for the language of the *Green Book* broadened almost immediately to embrace disapproval of the Book's theology and the multiple-choice nature of its services. Because championship of the Prayer Book's Tudor English was in their front window, they attracted to their ranks many who were emotionally attached to Prayer Book phrases. With the Society's threefold opposition to the revision, its membership grew rapidly. There were "well in excess of 30,000" by the time of the 1973 Convention when SPBCP was a little over two years old. By September 1976 they were claiming 100,000. It is not surprising that some persons who shared the Society's views were in the membership of the Prayer Book Revision Committees of the General Convention in their pre-Convention meetings in

Minneapolis. A reporter (for those three days of meetings were open to the press and the public) observed that "by calm answers and careful explanations [other members] were able to win over even the most stubborn opposition."[7]

"Careful explanations" were the Society's downfall. For oftentimes throughout the Convention, SPBCP members were shrill and emotional and did not have all the facts.

There were two evenings of Prayer Book hearings before the subject came to the House of Deputies for consideration. They were evenings of ventilation but not conversion. When Rite I was called "a careful edition of the 1928 Rite," its opponents responded, "It has been so tinkered with that it is not the same Rite." The opponents to the *Draft Proposed Book* played their tune in various keys, but always on the three strings of the SPBCP bow: it lacks the elevated language of the present Book; the proliferation of services will destroy the unity of the Church; the theology of Prayer Books 1549–1928 is being watered down. At the opposite end of the pendulum swing, proponents sang the praises of the Standing Liturgical Commission and testified to their experiences with the use of the *Green Book* and *Authorized Services*.

Three days later the House of Deputies began its two-day consideration of the *Draft Proposed Book*. During the interim, the Prayer Book Revision Committees of the two Houses of the Convention had worked, sometimes around the clock, making about one thousand changes in the *Draft Proposed Book*. They had listened to all that had been said from every quarter about the *Blue Book* and had taken seriously what they heard. Later in the Convention, Bishop Chilton Powell, Chairman of the Standing Liturgical Commission, said, "It's the people's book; not the expert's." He was right.

In the debate in the House of Deputies, members of the SPBCP led the fight to stop the Proposed Book or at least to include in it portions of the 1928 Book. As in the Prayer Book evening hearings, opponents of revision were sometimes shrill, but the Reverend Harold F. Lemoine, Chairman of the Prayer Book Committee and the presenter of the Committee's report, and Standing Liturgical Commission members on the floor, always responded in an open and sympathetic way, and with all the background information anyone could ask. Their attitude as well as the thoroughness with which they had done their job was impressive. There was genuine listening and real concern for those who anticipated loss of the 1928 Book as a disaster. Some three dozen last-minute amendments were made, seeking mainly to restore some parts and phrases of the 1928 Book. Most of these were defeated overwhelmingly by a patient House. One of the spectators in the crowded visitors' gallery was overheard observing:

I have been a priest for eight years and this is the first General Convention I have attended. It is evident to me that this House really wants this *Proposed Book*. It is not being forced on anyone. They really respect the work done by the Standing Liturgical Commission and accept it.

The House vote was taken Saturday evening at the end of a 10-hour day—95% of the clerical Deputies favored the Proposed Book, 80% of the lay Deputies. The House of Bishops in their turn voted almost unanimously for it.

The Proposed Book was authorized for use beginning the First Sunday of Advent, November 28, 1976. Printed copies of the new Book began reaching the congregations of the Church in February, 1977, an amazing four months after the General Convention. (The same process had taken almost a year in 1928–29.) This was achieved thanks to the Herculean efforts of the Office of the Coordinator of Prayer Book Revision, the Reverend Leo Malania, and his assistant, Captain Howard Galley, C.A., along with the superlative cooperation and assistance of The Church Hymnal Corporation, the publisher, whose president, Robert A. Robinson, and colleagues went far beyond the call of the publisher's role in their assistance.

As were its predecessors, the Proposed Book is both like the heritage from which it springs and different in noticeable ways. The first differences which cry out for justification are the proliferation of services and the use of what is to some disturbingly modern English. The Book is intended to be *common* prayer, and all Episcopalians are not attuned to sixteenth-century English. Actually that language is, as Marion Hatchett says, "inaccessible to some and distasteful to others." It is recognized that the traditional language is a symbol of our continuity with the past; it also meets a genuine pastoral need. On the other hand, contemporary phraseology is more appreciated and more attractive to many than Tudor English, and is for them a better medium through which Word and Sacraments are conveyed. Certainly those Episcopalians clothed only in the familiar garb of contemporary English should not be excluded from the banquet of the Lord's Word and Sacraments merely because they have not acquired the festal robes of Tudor English. Their needs must be met along with those of others, if the Book is to deserve the title "Common Prayer." As Bishop Parsons wrote over fifty years ago regarding parts of the 1928 Book, which was then still in labor:

Some variations in use must be permitted either because they are equally desirable on liturgical grounds or because they contribute to the catholic comprehensiveness of the Book.[8]

So the often-used services—Morning and Evening Prayer, the Holy Eucharist, and Burial—are in two versions. This is certainly not a move to replace Rite I (traditional language) with Rite II (contemporary language) and no one thinks this is ever likely to happen. It is intended to enable all worshippers to be at ease in using it.

And when services are couched in contemporary language, God is addressed as "You," which is shocking and distasteful to many. To such persons it is too chummy and intimate, even disrespectful. "Thou" had the quality of respect and reverence. But there are others who find that the intimate address "You" gives reality to their prayers. In Thomas Cranmer's day, "Thou" was the pronoun of intimacy, the language of love and religion. Today in French, Spanish and German, the intimate pronoun is used in religion as well as in love. The evolution of the English language from the sixteenth to the twentieth century had created a halo about the second person pronoun used in prayer. In order to translate the feeling and atmosphere of Cranmer's sixteenth-century devotions into present-day English, we must use "You."

There are other differences, many of which we notice as we look at the Book more closely. Here are some of them.

● The Title Page. It is essentially the same as previously, except for the word "Proposed" and the use of the name "The

Episcopal Church" instead of the longer official name. The Prayer Book is used not only in the United States but also in other independent countries where the name "The Protestant Episcopal Church in the United States of America" could be an embarrassment.

● Front Matter. Only the Calendar of the Church Year remains up front. This Calendar enhances the significance of Sunday and the feasts of our Lord over all the red and black letter Saints' days. The pre-Lenten "gesima" Sundays (a shadowy season of neither festival nor fast, dating from sixth century Roman practice) have been replaced by additional Sundays after Epiphany celebrating the revelation of Christ to the world. Thus revelation is built into the calendar along with incarnation, resurrection, and redemption. Another major change is the adoption of the more ancient practice of listing the Sundays of the latter half of the Church Year as "after Pentecost" rather than continuing to follow the practice which began in northern Europe in the late Middle Ages of designating them "after Trinity." This enhances emphasis on the importance of the great feast of Pentecost in the life of the Church. The necessary adjustment of the length of the season is now made at the beginning rather than at the end (rubric, page 158). This change insures an invariable pre-advent emphasis heralding the coming of God's Kingdom and a smooth transition into the new Church Year. The Lectionaries and other material which were formerly in front are now, more properly, in the back of the Book.

● The Daily Office. This section is expanded to include orders of worship for other times of day in addition to Morning and Evening Prayer and for individual and family devotions. There are two versions of both Morning and Evening Prayer: Rite I (traditional language) and Rite II (contemporary language). The form of Morning Prayer is essentially that of the 1928 service. There is greater latitude in the use of Canticles which can contribute to a more unified service. There are also two changes which were proposed back in 1922 but did not get into the 1928 Book. The first concerns the *Te Deum*; only two of the familiar three stanzas are here as was proposed then. Actually, stanza one is a hymn to the Holy Trinity, stanza two is a hymn to Christ, and the last is a series of suffrages which were later attached to the ancient hymn (earlier they had been attached to the *Gloria in excelsis*). The stanza which did not belong has been removed. The other 1922 proposal was made by Bishop Robert F. Gibson of Virginia, who urged that there be "a vigorous prayer for Missions" after the usual three Collects. The Bishop has finally been heard, and such a prayer is now obligatory.

● The Litany. This Tudor gem has undergone some felicitous rearranging for a better progression of thought; some wording has been enlighteningly modernized ("wickedness" instead of "mischief"), and some new petitions added, as, for example, "to preserve all who are in danger by reason of their labor or their travel," and petitions for the homeless and hungry, the lonely, the failing and infirm, and the faithful departed. Neither the flow, the dignity, nor the quality have been violated in the process.

● The Collects. Traditional/Contemporary. This section is placed here in order to be easily accessible to both the Daily Offices and the Eucharist in which the Collects are used. The texts of the appointed Lessons have not been printed for two reasons. Their inclusion would increase the size of the present book by 50%; and which of the nine authorized translations would be the arbitrary preference?

● Proper Liturgies for Special Days. These liturgies are truly a long-needed enrichment of the Prayer Book. They are for Ash Wednesday, Palm Sunday, Maundy Thursday, Good Friday, Holy Saturday, and the Great Vigil of Easter—occasions most of which every congregation celebrates and for which every parish priest formerly had to dig up appropriate material.

● Holy Baptism. This service is placed here because the two great Sacraments belong together. The rite is significantly different from that in the 1928 Book and a sharp break with traditional Anglican practice. Here is the reason. For a long time there had been dissatisfaction with the initiatory rites, Baptism and Confirmation, not only in America but throughout the Anglican Communion. The problem has both pastoral and theological dimensions. In seeking to deal with it creatively, the accent has changed from human depravity to the death and resurrection of our Lord and the gifts of the Spirit. (This shift began in the 1928 Book.) The ancient three-fold initiatory unity—Baptism, the Sealing with the Spirit, and First Communion—has also been restored. The Apostles' Creed, which is the Baptismal Creed, is used in its ancient interrogative form. The beautifully worded "Thanksgiving over the Water" is a considerable improvement over the arid ten words of previous Prayer Books. Since water is the important "outward and visible sign" of this Sacrament, it should receive this kind of greater significance. Both the Sponsors and the congregation are more actively involved in a rite which, when the candidate is not an infant, leads directly to joining in the eucharistic fellowship and commissioning for Christian mission. (See Confirmation below.)

● The Holy Eucharist. The new order of service conforms to that recommended by the Lambeth Conference in 1958. It was used in *The Liturgy of the Lord's Supper* in 1967 and has been retained because in trial use it had proven successful. Not only does this order conform to Early Church practice, it has been adopted by other churches of the Anglican Communion and the new Roman Catholic and Lutheran rites. The versatility of the service makes it conformable to the changing mood of the feasts and fasts of the Church Year. (This need was appreciated by Queen Victoria who once said to her chaplain that Easter is really too important and too happy a day to celebrate with a Prayer Book rite.[9]) There is a theological balance to the Eucharistic Prayers which was lost in 1892 when it was no longer obligatory to precede Holy Communion with Morning Prayer and the Litany. The doctrine of creation simply disappeared. It has been restored in the several Eucharistic Prayers of Rite II and in the alternate Great Thanksgiving of Rite I. The wording of the 1928 Service is preserved in Rite I with some updating of Elizabethan English. ("Thou dost vouchsafe to feed us" has become "Thou dost feed us.")

● Pastoral Offices. The significance of Confirmation has broadened and clarified. At Baptism all the gifts of the Spirit are imparted; Confirmation does not add to these. However, the Laying on of Hands is the rite of mature commitment to one's baptismal vows which had been made in one's behalf when

one was baptized as an infant. The psychological and peda-
gogical value of Confirmation is still present and prized. The
service is also appropriate for a person coming into the Episcopal Church from another Communion. He is already a full-
fledged Christian. His new commitment to the Episcopal Church
is here expressed before the Bishop. The service is also available
for a person entering a new phase of his or her life with Christ
or for one who has fallen away and is becoming active again.
The Marriage Service quite obviously makes the man and
woman equal partners, furthering an emphasis begun in the
1928 Book when "obey" was dropped from the woman's vow.
Scripture is read in the Service and the congregation is a great
deal more vocally involved. Then there are several much-needed
new services—the Blessing of a Civil Marriage, Thanksgiving
for the Adoption of a Child, Reconciliation of a Penitent, and
Commitment to Christian Service. The Ministration to the Sick
has been usably revised. It thoughtfully includes a section of
Prayers for use *by* a Sick Person. It is followed by Ministration
at the Time of Death. How pastors have needed such Prayer
Book assistance when they have shared the long night watches
with waiting loved ones! The Burial Office, Rites I and II,
has been enriched with more optional Readings and more
Psalms, and the resurrection is unquestionably central. This
change in emphasis from awe in the presence of death and the
fear of judgment to the joy of the resurrection began in the
1928 Book.

● Episcopal Services. These are services which require a bishop
as celebrant. In addition to the Ordination Services and a
service for the Consecration of a Church or Chapel, there is
the Celebration of a New Ministry. This last replaces the former
Institution of Ministers and lends itself to wider use.

● The Psalter. This new translation of the Psalms upsets many
people in part at least because they have the old phraseology
embedded in their memories and these new sounds are discordant. The translation was done by biblical scholars, poets,
and musicians. It achieves clarity by using quotation marks
to indicate direct speech (Ps. 46), spacing between sections of
Psalms (Ps. 51), rephrasing obscure passages (Ps. 49:7-9), and
removing misleading male sex references (Ps. 1). In the process,

Psalms whose meaning and beauty were overlooked have taken on new brilliance (Ps. 99). Of course nothing can replace the noble beauty of some of the Tudor Psalms (Ps. 23), but the Psalter is intended to be a vehicle of intelligible worship, which much of the sixteenth-century version had ceased to be for many people. There is a difference between a literary society and a worshipping congregation, and the day comes when "Time makes ancient good uncouth." This fact comes hard for those of us who have that "ancient good" chiseled on our memories.

● Prayers and Thanksgivings. This section, which formerly followed The Daily Office, has been indexed and enlarged. It is therefore more versatile and easier to use.

● An Outline of the Faith or Catechism. This new section gives laymen a rather thorough outline of Christian belief. It is considerably more comprehensive than the old Catechism, which was chiefly a brief treatment of the Creed, Lord's Prayer and Ten Commandments, the catechetical necessity for children before they might be confirmed.

● Historical Documents of the Church. Here are five significant documents which have milestone importance in the history of Christian thought and which the layman might otherwise only know by name. They are: Definition of the Union of the Divine and Human Natures in the Person of Christ, Council of Chalcedon, 451 A.D.; The Creed of Saint Athanasius; Preface, The First Book of Common Prayer (1549); Articles of Religion; and The Chicago-Lambeth Quadrilateral 1886, 1888.

● The Lectionary. The Word of God has come into greater prominence and more thorough use than in any previous Prayer Book. Scriptures are read on a three-year cycle, Old Testament lessons and psalms have been restored to the eucharistic rites, and almost all services now have provisions for the reading and exposition of the Word. It is true that the power of hearing the same Epistle and Gospel on a given Sunday year after year has been lost. But this has more than been compensated for by the fact that a considerably larger range of Scripture is used. Add to this the fact that the Sunday Lectionary conforms closely to that used by the Roman Catholic, Lutheran, Presbyterian,

United Church of Christ and Methodist Churches. As we saw above, the order of service in the Eucharist is widely used by other Churches. Now we see that the contents of the Lectionary are also widely used. This means that the rank-and-file members of the Christian Church find their common life in gathering around the Lord's Table—the ecumenical thrust of the 1970s.

● Daily Office Lectionary. This table in a two-part cycle has been completely revised to complement the Sunday Lectionary.

It may be too early to know except in a general way how the Proposed Book is being received by the Church. The immediate reaction at the Minneapolis Convention was elation among its proponents and gloom among those who opposed it. Bishop Powell took a measured view of its adoption:

The Church must experience this book. If anyone wants to stop it, they can stop it next time. The point is we cannot know the book by reading it, but only by using those forms to offer our duty to God.

Professor Harold L. Weatherby, Secretary of SPBCP, in analyzing their efforts to swing sentiment away from the Proposed Book said, "We made no converts." The Rev. Richard W. Ingalls, president of the Foundation for Christian Theology, suggesting something nefarious, wrote in *The Christian Challenge* that "the Society...faced a more determined and brutal opposition at the General Convention than they had anticipated."[10] To this day, members of the SPBCP are convinced that the Book was "put over" by the mammoth lobbying effort of a small group of its champions. At convention time they were apparently unaware of the avalanche of pre-convention mail which had virtually assured its passage. Even those who favored it were surprised at the size of the vote. Actually, the Book sold itself.

In the Church at large, the most extreme reaction against the Proposed Book was that of some persons who left the Episcopal Church. A few of these, like some of the leadership of the SPBCP, took this step because of Prayer Book revision. However, most of those who defected since General Convention had a fistful of grievances—the ordination of women, the homosexuality controversy, and others—as well as their objection to the Proposed Prayer Book. About a year after General Convention, *The Living Church* reported that the Diocesan Press Service survey showed 18 congregations had voted to withhold funds, 10 had declined Episcopal visitations, and 13 had voted to leave the Episcopal Church. The total number of people who had withdrawn from the Episcopal Church by the end of 1977 was about 3,000 out of an estimated 2.9 million. Since that time their numbers have increased somewhat and they have organized as the Anglican Church of North America. How strong this dissident group will ultimately be is not predictable. There was a previous disgruntled splinter group in the 1870s which became the Reformed Episcopal Church. The issue then was churchmanship. They made the Proposed Prayer Book of 1786 their official Book. A hundred years have passed and they have 6,532 members in 64 congregations.

A year after the 1976 Convention the Rev. Mr. Ingalls was darkly prophesying the Proposed Book's derailment in *The Christian Challenge*:

It is little wonder that some previously enthusiastic supporters of the Proposed Book are now finding it to be sickly stale. The novelty has worn off. . . . To be rid of the literary qualities of the 1549–1928 Book of Common Prayer is worse than vulgarizing Shakespeare. . . . If a churchwide referendum were held, the 1928 Book of Common Prayer would win in a landslide over the Proposed Book.[11]

Such a sweeping statement does not square with the impression one gets from around the country.

There has been no churchwide survey and probably there will be none. But when the diocesan chairmen of liturgical commissions met in Shreveport in November, 1977, the general feeling among them was that the Book is taken for granted. Bishops and clergy throughout the Church are slowly digesting, appropriating, and coming to feel at home with the Book. One diocesan commission chairman in his annual report to his diocese stated that

the majority of laypersons have found the transition to the Proposed Book far less traumatic than they had feared, and indeed, most feel that the services are faithful to the tradition of the 1928 Prayer Book.

He concluded with the observation that "the majority of lay-persons no longer see the matter of the Prayer Book, old or new, as an overriding issue."[12] This seems to be true for a large number of church people, clergy and lay. The adoption of the Proposed Book is no longer a live issue, except with the SPBCP whose leadership was shattered by the action of General Convention. There is now a great deal of lethargy. After all, matters of liturgical practice have been a primary concern of the Church for a decade. People get tired. This was true in 1889. Nine years of Prayer Book deliberation were enough; the passage of the Book in 1892 was taken for granted. It was true in 1925. The process had begun back in 1913. The Church had had enough; passage of the 1928 Book was assumed. History seems to be repeating itself. *The Living Church* is probably correct: "It is widely anticipated that the proposed book will become the Book of Common Prayer."[13]

At the same time there has been increasing concern for "the distressed people of the Church," as the Presiding Bishop, John M. Allin, calls them, who find the switch to a new Book more than they can handle. This concern began expressing itself as soon as the Proposed Book passed the two Houses of General Convention, and it crystallized in a joint commission to make a recommendation regarding continued use of the 1928 Book beyond 1979 should the Proposed Book be ratified. Bishop Allin has steadfastly championed this cause. In his address to the 1976 General Convention he said, "It is my hope that people who still prefer the present Prayer Book will be able to experience worship as they are accustomed, even if a newer version is adopted." And a year later he urged the House of Bishops at their meeting in Port St. Lucie, Florida, "Once again I plead with you to give such assurance [*i.e.*, "that the Prayer Book of 1928 shall continue to be available for use"] and make proper provision graciously. . . ." Letters in the Church press argue that this permission to continue the use of the 1928 Book will be a divisive element in the Church. Proponents of that permissive use employ the same argument as a way to avoid possible division. The 1979 General Convention will determine what course of action will be followed.

Among the individual responses to the Proposed Book which have come our way are those of two elderly *grandes dames* of the Church, who happen to live on opposite coasts. The eastern lady writes:

There are times when I welcome an old Prayer Book service with its familiar and restful rhythms, but I wouldn't go back if we had to lose some of the new services—like . . . the one that solemnized a civil marriage ceremony . . . and then there was the service of making a commitment to care for an adopted child within the church community. Each of these has been thrilling and *right,* and wouldn't have been shared with the congregation in the old days. So there I stand.

Her California counterpart confides:

I was baptized using the Prayer Book of 1790. I was confirmed and married using the Prayer Book of 1892. I have helped rear my children using the Prayer Book of 1928, and I can't wait to take part in services from the Prayer Book of 1979.

So the story is incomplete. Like the 97-year-old California lady, we shall just have to wait. The journey is not over. The Proposed Book ventured out of the safe fortress of Prayer Book Studies and for a decade has traversed the craggy mountains of trial use and the scorching sands of criticism. It was strengthened and vitalized by its stay at the oasis in Minneapolis and is now within a year of its goal. Will that be the end of the journey or will it be the real beginning?

CHAPTER X

Prospective—Looking Forward

The Prefaces of the Prayer Books of Edward VI (1549 and 1552) and the Acts of Uniformity which made them official make it clear that the Book of Common Prayer is accountable to three fundamental criteria. It is "grounded upon the holy scriptures," "agreeable to the order of the primitive church," and expected to be edifying to the people. These have hovered like seraphim over the deliberators who have produced every succeeding revision of the Prayer Book.

The extent to which earlier revisions have been loyal to these hovering imperatives and the cloud of worshippers past who honored them is academic. Our investment is in the present, and in the Proposed Book. Does it measure up? Does it have those innate Prayer Book qualities which make it the real thing? In other words, is the Proposed Book of 1976 a continuation of or a departure from Prayer Book tradition? Let us consider those three criteria.

Biblical theology and a renewed emphasis on Holy Scriptures have undergone a renaissance since the 1928 revision. The Proposed Book reflects its effects to such an extent that a complete listing would be tedious. Here are some major examples:

● The Lectionary is fuller. Several times more Scripture is heard in the regular services than was the case with the 1928 Book.

● In every service Scripture is read and there is opportunity for exposition. In 1928 and previous books, there is no rubrical provision for a sermon in Morning and Evening Prayer, or in any of the so-called Occasional Offices. The Proposed Book takes it for granted that a sermon will be preached at every celebration of the Eucharist. It is not just an option. There is also a provision for a sermon at Morning and Evening Prayer.

● The full Scriptural emphasis has been recovered in the Eucharistic Prayers. All of them, except the Canon from the 1928 Book in Rite I, now proclaim God as creator, give thanks for the incarnation, as well as the crucifixion, proclaim the resurrection and point to the messianic banquet, as well as recalling the Last Supper.

● The biblical references are restored to the Baptismal Rite, especially in the Thanksgiving over the Water.

● Easter is celebrated with a new wealth of Scripture at the vigil, even more than was in the 1549 and 1552 Books.

● Misquotations of Scripture have been corrected (*e.g.*, the Prayer of St. Chrysostom), and its misuse eliminated (*e.g.*, the Acts reading at Confirmation in the 1928 Book).

● There is a renewed biblical emphasis on the Holy Spirit, the Church, and the nature of Sunday, throughout the Book.

Yes, the Proposed Book is "grounded upon the holy scriptures." This is a return to the intent of Thomas Cranmer and his colleagues, which the previous American books had let slide.

Now consider the extent to which the Book is "agreeable to the order of the primitive church." Liturgical scholars agree that we know infinitely more about the Early Church and its liturgy than Cranmer could possibly have known. Many ancient documents were not even known to exist in his day. As a result of this new knowledge, there is a new emphasis on the Great Fifty Days of the Easter-Pentecost season. Lent is now seen as a time of preparation for Baptism and of renewal of one's Baptismal vows, and the Easter Vigil as a principal time for baptisms. There is a recovery of the traditional and pastoral functions of various orders of ministers. This rubric is a result of the new awareness of, and, to as great an extent as possible, a return to the liturgical practice of the Early Church:

In all services, the entire Christian assembly participates in such a way that the members of each order within the Church, lay persons, bishops, priests, and deacons, fulfill the functions proper to their respective orders, as set forth in the rubrical directions for each service. (p. 13)

This listing of primitive Church influence could also be extended.

The third ancient Prayer Book criterion is the edifying of the people. The occasions on which the Proposed Book teaches those who use it are numerous. Here are some of them: the Proper Liturgies for Special Days, the provision for a homily or sermon at every service, the Baptismal Service which involves the worshipping congregation, the learning which accompanies lay participation in the conduct of services, the amount of Holy Scripture which is heard by congregations in the enlightening context of the season or service, such as Marriage and Burial, and the more broadly based Catechism. These are among the ways in which edifying the people takes on new significance.

We conclude that evaluated by the three criteria Thomas Cranmer has bequeathed to us, the Proposed Book is a continuation of and not a departure from our venerable Prayer Book tradition.

In another, less profound way this present Book is in step with its predecessors. The objections to it are almost identical with those leveled at former revisions.

"The language is . . . not up to the standard of the old Book." (1886)

"There is a vital change in our doctrinal position." (1919)

"There is a bewildering quantity of 'or this's.'" (1885)

"In this so-called revision the Book is changed . . . so radically as to be hardly recognized." (1919)

The Society for the Preservation of the Book of Common Prayer has forefathers who complained in almost the same language about changes which the Society defends today. These ancestors sometimes even used the Society's own words to oppose the Book now precious to their children. Opposition to Prayer Book revision often plays the same tune in every generation, and behind rational reasoning is the basic human resistance to changing comfortable, familiar words the meanings of which our emotions do not bother to analyze. All of us cherish "the *comfortable* gospel of Christ" with which the charlatans of change should not dare to tamper. "The holy ground of the Prayer Book I love should not be desecrated by those who refuse to take off the shoes of scholarly research and relevance to the times."

All of us feel this way to some degree, in unguarded moments.

The Prayer Book has benefited from the genuine loyalty of those who are hurt by revision. Indeed, that loyalty has contributed to every revision of the Book. For each Prayer Book in its turn has made its contribution to the worshipping church people of its day partly because the chargers of change could not be held back, and partly because the reins of restraint prevented a tragic runaway.

Revision was always anticipated to be germane to the genius of the Book of Common Prayer. Cranmer's Preface to the first two Prayer Books opens with the words:

There was never anything by the wit of man so well devised, or so sure established, which in continuance of time hath not been corrupted, as (among other things) it may plainly appear by the common prayers in the Church.

The framers of our first American Prayer Book shared the same spirit, as their Preface (which is still a part of our Book) indicates:

It is a most invaluable part of that blessed "liberty wherewith Christ hath made us free," that in his worship different forms and usages may without offence be allowed ... as may seem most convenient for the edification of the people, "according to the various exigency of times and occasions."

The General Convention of 1892 was also aware of the loose ends with which their revision had not come to grips. And, as we have seen, the Convention of 1928 saw Prayer Book revision as a recurring necessity (page 80). It is not surprising that the Standing Liturgical Commission in its report to the 1976 Convention shared this same view about the ultimate need for revision.

The recognition by the General Convention that the central Book of worship of the Church cannot be allowed to become out-dated makes it necessary for the Liturgical Commission to be prepared to present to the General Convention, at reasonable intervals of, say, fifteen or twenty years, major suggestions for further revision of the Prayer Book. This, in fact, is the continuing responsibility which the Standing Liturgical Commission has been established to discharge.[1]

The Prayer Book must never be treated like bronzed baby shoes—frozen in an age, unchangeable, precious. Rather it is precious because it is an instrument responsive to the needs of each succeeding generation of worshippers as well as the treasury of spiritual gems they will prize and use to adorn their advent into the presence of the Most High.

We began with the question, what is the *real* Prayer Book? Now that we are more conversant with that Book's often stormy trip through the centuries, perhaps we are more competent to answer or at least more appreciative of the answer given. It is almost miraculous that each succeeding Book has been able to stand with confidence before the three dicta which, like a judicial tribunal, have passed judgment on its worthiness—grounded in Scripture, attuned to Early Church practice, and edifying to the people. At the same time part of the strength of the Prayer Book is its solemn language inherited from past centuries, yet never allowed to become out-dated. This combination of qualities we identify with the real Prayer Book.

But in a canonical sense you and I do not have the final voice. John W. Suter, Jr., who was Custodian of the Book of Common Prayer from 1942 to 1962, was once asked, "What is the Standard Book of Common Prayer?" (That is, what is *the* official Book of Common Prayer to which all currently-used Prayer Books must conform?) He replied, "It is whatever the General Convention says it is at the moment the question is asked."[2]

The Changeless and the Changing Prayer Book

(Excerpts from a sermon preached by Doctor William Reed Huntington in All Saints' Church, Worcester, Massachusetts, following the 1880 General Convention.*)

As there were heroes before Agamemnon, so there were holy and humble men of heart before Cranmer and Luther—yes, and before Jerome and Augustine. If any cry that ever went up from any one of them out of the depths of that nature which they share with us and we with them; if any breath of supplication, any mourn of penitence, any shout of victory that issued from their lips has made out to survive the noise and tumult of intervening times, it has earned by its very persistency of tone a *prima facie* title to be put in the Prayer Book of today.

A prayer book holds the utterances of our needs; a theological system is the embodiment of our thoughts. Now, our thoughts about things divine are painfully fallible and liable to change with change of times; but a want which is genuinely and entirely human is a permanent fact. The great needs of the soul never grow obsolete; and although the language in which the lips shall clothe the heart's desire may alter, as tastes alter, yet the substance of the prayer abides, and in some happy instances, the form also abides.

The past of the Common Prayer we cannot disconnect from England, but its present and its future belong in part at least to us, and it is in this light that we are bound as American Churchmen to study them.

What we have to fear is that during the long delay which puts off the only proper and regular method of giving more elasticity to the services, there may spring up a generation of

---

Churchmen from whose minds the idea of obligation to law in matters of ritual observance will have faded out altogether.

[He dreamed of the day when there would be] a revision undertaken not for the purpose of giving victory to one theological party rather than to another, or of changing in any degree the doctrinal teaching of the Church, but solely and wholly with a view of enriching, amplifying, and making more available the liturgical treasures of the book.

We are bound, with the changed times, to provide for the new wants, new satisfactions.

We must remember that the men who gave us what we now have were, in their day and generation, the innovators, advocates of what the more timid spirits accounted dangerous change. We cannot, I think, sufficiently admire the courageous foresight of those reformers who, at a time when public worship was mainly associated in men's minds with what went on among a number of ecclesiastics gathered at one end of a church, dared to plant themselves firmly on the principle of "common" prayer, and say, Henceforth the worship of the national Church shall be the worship, not of priests alone, but of priests and people too. What a bold act it was!

No Churchman questions the wisdom of their innovations now. Is it hopeless to expect a like quickness of discernment in the leaders of today? Surely they have eyes to see that a new world has been born, and that a thousand unexampled demands are pressing us on every side.

The true way to better things is always to begin by holding on manfully to that which we already are convinced is good. The best restorers of old buildings are those who work with affectionate loyalty as nearly as possible on the line of the first builders, averse to any change which is made merely for change's sake, not so anxious to modernize as to restore, and yet always awake to the fact that what they have been set to do is to make the building once more what it was first meant to be, a practical shelter.

Notes

Chapter One, facing page

1. G. J. Cuming, *A History of Anglican Liturgy* (London: Macmillan & Co., Ltd.; New York: St. Martin's Press, 1969), 49, with permission.
2. *Ibid.*, 13.

Chapter Two

1. Marion J. Hatchett, *Sanctifying Life, Time and Space—An Introduction to Liturgical Study*, "A Crossroad Book" (New York: The Seabury Press, 1976), 113, with permission.
2. There are two convocations—Canterbury and York. These bodies along with Parliament enact legislation for the Church including the designation of the official Book of Common Prayer.
3. Francis Procter and Walter Howard Frere, *A New History of the Book of Common Prayer* (Revised ed. 1901; London: Macmillan & Company, Ltd., 1955), 50, with permission.
4. Percy Dearmer, *The Story of the Prayer Book in the Old and New World and Throughout the Anglican Church* (London: Oxford University Press, 1958), 57, with permission.
5. Cuming, *op. cit.*, 86.
6. *Ibid.*, 81.
7. Procter and Frere, *op. cit.*, 66.
8. *Ibid.*, 56.
9. Cuming, *op. cit.*, 103.
10. Procter and Frere, *op. cit.*, 83–85.
11. Dearmer, *op. cit.*, 70.
12. *Ibid.*, 71.

Chapter Three

1. John E. Booty (ed.), *The Book of Common Prayer 1559—The Elizabethan Prayer Book* (Washington, D.C.: Folger Shakespeare Library, 1976), 332, with permission.
2. Dearmer, *op. cit.*, 78.
3. Cuming, *op. cit.*, 128.
4. Dearmer, *op. cit.*, 81.

5. Procter and Frere, *op. cit.*, 104–5.
6. *Ibid.*, 113.
7. Cuming, *op. cit.*, 128.
8. *Ibid.*, 135.
9. Booty, *op. cit.*, 330.

Chapter Four

1. Cuming, *op. cit.*, 139.
2. Dearmer, *op. cit.*, 90.
3. *Ibid.*, 91.
4. Cuming, *op. cit.*, 145.

Chapter Five

1. Cuming, *op. cit.*, 151; Procter and Frere, *op. cit.*, 163.
2. Cuming, *op. cit.*, 154.
3. Booty, *op. cit.*, 329.

Chapter Six

1. Marion J. Hatchett, "The Making of the First American Prayer Book" (unpublished Th.D. dissertation, General Theological Seminary, New York, 1972), 100.
2. A. Dean Calcote, "The Proposed Prayer Book of 1785," *The Historical Magazine of the Protestant Episcopal Church*, XLVI (September, 1977), 285.
3. Such books as *The Book of Common Prayer Reformed According to the Plan of the Late Dr. Samuel Clarke*, 1774; *Free and Candid Disquisitations*, anonymous, 1749; *The Expediency and Necessity of Revision and Improving the Publick Liturgy*, anonymous, 1749. See Hatchett, "First American Prayer Book," 67–79.
4. Calcote, *op. cit.*, 291.
5. Hatchett, "First American Prayer Book," 210.
6. Calcote, *op. cit.*, 294; Hatchett, "First American Prayer Book," 211.
7. Hatchett, "First American Prayer Book," 234.
8. *Ibid.*, 221, 241–43, and 440n52.
9. Calcote, *op. cit.*, 291.
10. Quoted by Hatchett, "First American Prayer Book," 280, from George W. Corner (ed.), *The Autobiography of Benjamin Rush* (Philadelphia: American Philosophical Society, 1948), 165.
11. Hatchett, "First American Prayer Book," 316.

Chapter Seven

1. Hatchett, "First American Prayer Book," 313.
2. *The Churchman*, XLII (November 20, 1880), editorial.

3. *Ibid.*, November 6, 1880, editorial.
4. *The Living Church*, V (September 22, 1883), editorial.
5. *Ibid.*, November 3, 1883, editorial.
6. *The Southern Churchman*, November 8, 1883.
7. *The Living Church*, VIII (February 27, 1886; July 11 and 4, 1885).
8. Annual Council Address, 1885, *ibid.*, VIII (June 27, 1885).
9. *Ibid.*, November 28, 1885. Letter to the Editor.
10. *The Churchman*, LIV (September 25, 1886), editorial.
11. *The Living Church*, XII (July 20, 1889).
12. *The Churchman*, LX (November 2, 1889).
13. *The Hymnal 1940 Companion.* Prepared by the Joint Commission on the Revision of the Hymnal of the Protestant Episcopal Church in the United States of America (New York: The Church Pension Fund: 1949), xix–xxiv.
14. Hatchett, "First American Prayer Book," 314.

Chapter Eight

1. *The Living Church*, XLIX (October 25, 1913), quotation from Convention Journal.
2. *The Churchman*, CXIV (October 7, 1916), Letter to the Editor.
3. *Ibid.*, November 4, 1916, editorial.
4. *The Southern Churchman*, LXXXIV (August 30, September 20, October 11, 1919); *The Living Church*, LXI (October 18, 1919). Letters to the Editor.
5. *The Churchman*, CXX (November 15, 1919).
6. *Ibid.*, September 6, 1919, Letter to the Editor.
7. *The Living Church*, LXVII (September 9, 1922).
8. *Ibid.*, September 23, 1922; *The Witness*, VII (September 16, 1922).
9. *The Witness*, VII (October 7, 1922), editorial.
10. *The Southern Churchman*, LXXXVII (October 21, 1922), Letter to the Editor.
11. *The Churchman*, CXXXII (September 22, 1925).
12. *Ibid.*, November 11, 1925, editorial.
13. *The Living Church*, LXXIII (September 19, 1925), editorial.
14. *Ibid.*, October 3, 1925, Letter to the Editor.
15. *Ibid.*
16. *Ibid.*, October 17, 1925, editorial.
17. *The Churchman*, CXXXVIII (November 3, 1928), Letter to the Editor.
18. *The Witness*, XIII (October 18, 1928).
19. *The Journal of the General Convention of the Protestant Episcopal Church in the U.S.A.*, October 10–25, 1928, Washington, D.C., p. 472.
20. *Ibid.*, 352.
21. *Ibid.*, 107.

22. *The Southern Churchman,* XCIII (October 6, 1928), Letter to the Editor.

23. *The Living Church,* LXXXI (June 15, 1929), Letter to the Editor.

24. *The Witness,* XIV (November 30, 1929).

Chapter Nine

1. Cuming, *op. cit.,* 248.

2. *Journal of General Convention,* October 11–23, 1964, St. Louis, Missouri, p. 348.

3. Cuming, *op. cit.,* 249.

4. *Journal of General Convention,* September 11–23, 1976, Minneapolis, Minnesota, p. 221.

5. *Ibid.,* 223.

6. SPBCP Newsletter, No. 19, Early Trinity, signed by Walter Sullivan.

7. *The Newsletter of Associated Parishes,* October, 1976, p. 2.

8. *The Southern Churchman,* LXXXVII (June 10, 1922).

9. Marion J. Hatchett, "The New Book: A Continuation of or Departure from the Tradition," *The Newsletter of the Associated Parishes,* June, 1977, p. 9.

10. *The Christian Challenge,* XVI, January, 1977.

11. *Ibid.,* October, 1977.

12. Report of Chairman Robt. C. Hall, Jr., to the 183rd Annual Council of the Diocese of Virginia, Fredericksburg, Virginia, February 10, 1978.

13. *The Living Church,* CLXXVI (January 22, 1978).

Chapter Ten

1. *Journal of General Convention,* 1976, p. 224.

2. *Journal of General Convention,* 1964, p. 446.

Selected Bibliography

Unpublished Document:

Marion J. Hatchett, "The Making of the First American Prayer Book."
Unpublished Th.D. dissertation, General Theological Seminary,
New York, New York, 1972. Copyright 1973.

Editions of the Book of Common Prayer:

*The Book of Common Prayer and Administration of the Sacraments
and Other Rites and Ceremonies of the Church of England.* 1604.
London: William Pickering, 1844. Reprint.

*The Book of Common Prayer and Administration of the Sacraments
and Other Rites and Ceremonies According to the use of the
Church of England together with The Psalter or Psalms of David
pointed as they are to be sung or said in Churches and the Form
or Manner of Making Ordaining and Consecrating of Bishops
Priests and Deacons.* 1662. Reprint. Cambridge: At the University Press, no date.

*The Book of Common Prayer, and Administration of the Sacraments,
and Other Rites and Ceremonies of the Church, According to
the use of the Church of England; together with The Psalter
or Psalms of David, Pointed as they are to be sung and said in
Churches; And the Form and Manner of Making, Ordaining,
and Consecrating Bishops, Priests, and Deacons.* 1662. Reprint.
Published in the United States and Canada by W. Walter Dunne,
of number one hundred and thirty-five, Fifth Avenue, New York,
under a joint arrangement with the Essex Press of Camden,
Gloucestershire, England, The Guild of Handicraft, London,
England, and the Messrs. Eyre & Spottiswoode, Printers to his
Majesty King Edward VII, no date.

*The Book of Common Prayer and Administration of the Sacraments
and Other Rites and Ceremonies according to the use of the
Protestant Episcopal Church in the United States of America
together with The Psalter or Psalms of David.* 1790. Reprint.
Philadelphia: J. B. Lippincott & Co., 1850.

Idem. New York: Thomas Nelson and Sons, 1892.

Idem. New York: Thomas Nelson and Sons, 1944.

The Book of Common Prayer according to the use of The Reformed Episcopal Church in the United States of America. Same as the Proposed Prayer Book of 1785. Philadelphia: The Reformed Episcopal Publication Society, Ltd., 1930.

Proposed The Book of Common Prayer and Administration of the Sacraments and other Rites and Ceremonies of the Church Together with The Psalter or Psalms of David According to the use of the Episcopal Church. 1976. New York: The Church Hymnal Corporation and The Seabury Press, 1977.

Journals of General Convention:

Journal of the General Convention of the Protestant Episcopal Church. Meeting in Baltimore, October 5–25, 1892. Printed for the Convention, 1893.

Idem. Meeting in Minneapolis, October 2–22, 1895. Printed for the Convention, 1896.

Idem. Meeting in Portland, Oregon, September 6–23, 1922. Printed for the Convention, 1923.

Idem. Meeting in New Orleans, October 7–24, 1925. Printed for the Convention, 1926.

Idem. Meeting in Washington, D.C., October 10–25, 1928. Printed for the Convention, 1929.

Idem. Meeting in Denver, Colorado, September 16–30, 1931. Printed for the Convention, 1932.

Idem. Meeting in St. Louis, Missouri, October 11–23, 1964. Printed for the Convention, 1964.

Idem. Meeting in Seattle, September 17–27, 1967. Printed for the Convention, 1968.

Idem. Meeting in Houston, October 11–22, 1970. Printed for the Convention, 1970.

Idem. Meeting in Louisville, Kentucky, September 26–October 11, 1973. Printed for the Convention, 1974.

Idem. Meeting in Minneapolis, September 11–23, 1976. Printed for the Convention, 1977.

Periodicals:

The Christian Challenge (Victoria, Texas: The Foundation for Christian Theology), XVI (1977).

The Churchman (New York: M. H. Mallory Co.), XLII (1880), LIV (1886), LX (1889); (New York: The Churchman Publishing Co.), CXIV (1916), CXX (1919), CXXXII (1925), CXXXVIII (1928).

The Historical Magazine of the Protestant Episcopal Church (Detroit: Gale Research Co.), XLVI (September, 1977).

The Living Church (Milwaukee: The Young Churchman Co.), V (1882–83), VIII (1885–86), XII (1889–90), XLIX (1912–13)

LXI (1918–19), LXVII (1922), LXXIII (1925); (Milwaukee: The Living Church Foundation, Inc.), CLXXVI (1978).

The Newsletter of the Associated Parishes (Alexandria, Virginia), 1976, 1977.

The Southern Churchman (Richmond, Virginia: The Southern Churchman Co.), XLIX (1883), LXXXIV (1919), LXXXVII (1922).

The Witness (Chicago: The Witness Publishing Co.), VII (1922), XIII (1928).

Other Works:

The Book Annexed to the Report of the Joint Committee on the *Book of Common Prayer* as modified by the Action of the General Convention of 1883. New York: E. & J. B. Young & Co., 1885.

John E. Booty (ed.), *The Book of Common Prayer 1559—The Elizabethan Prayer Book.* Washington, D.C.: Folger Shakespeare Library, 1976.

F. E. Brightman, *The English Rite Being a Synopsis of the Sources and Revisions of the Book of Common Prayer with an Introduction and an Appendix.* 2 Volumes. London: Rivingtons, 1915.

A. Dean Calcote, "The Proposed Prayer Book of 1785," *Historical Magazine of the Protestant Episcopal Church*, XLVI (1977), 275–95.

G. J. Cuming, *A History of Anglican Liturgy.* London: Macmillan and Co., Ltd.; New York: St. Martin's Press, Inc., 1969.

Percy Dearmer, *The Story of the Prayer Book in the Old and New World and Throughout the Anglican Church.* Based upon the Author's *Everyman's History of the Prayer Book.* First edition 1933. Reprint. London: Oxford University Press, 1933.

John Dowden, *The Scottish Communion Office 1764 with Introduction, History of the Office and Appendices.* New Edition seen through the Press by H. A. Wilson. Oxford: At the Clarendon Press, 1922.

The First and Second Prayer Books of Edward VI. Introduction by The Rt. Rev. E. C. S. Gibson (Everyman's Library, No. 448). New York: E. P. Dutton & Co., 1910.

Marion J. Hatchett, *Sanctifying Life, Time and Space—An Introduction to Liturgical Study* (A Crossroad Book). New York: The Seabury Press, 1976.

William R. Huntington, *The Book Annexed: Its Critics and Its Prospects.* Three papers reprinted from *The Church Review.* New York: 1886.

————, *A Short History of The Book of Common Prayer together with Certain Papers Illustrative of Liturgical Revision, 1878–1892.* New York: Thomas Whittaker, 1893.

The Hymnal 1940 Companion. Prepared by the Joint Commission on the Revision of the Hymnal of the Protestant Episcopal Church in the United States of America. New York: The Church Pension Fund, 1949.

The Liturgy of the Lord's Supper: A Revision of Prayer Book Studies IV. (Prayer Book Studies XVII, The Standing Liturgical Commission of the Protestant Episcopal Church in the United States of America.) New York: The Church Pension Fund, 1966.

William McGarvey, *Liturgiae Americanae or The Book of Common Prayer as used in the United States of America compared with the Proposed Book of 1786 and with the Prayer Book of The Church of England and an Historical Account and Documents. To which is added a Bibliographical Sketch of the Standard Editions of the Amercian Prayer Book, and a Critical Examination of the Prayer Book Psalter, by the Rev. Frederick Gibson, D. D.* Philadelphia: Limited Edition of 1000, 1895. Copy No. 999.

Edward Lambe Parsons and Bayard Hale Jones, *The American Prayer Book—Its Origins and Principles.* New York: Charles Scribner's Sons, 1946.

Prayers We Have in Common. Agreed Liturgical Texts proposed by The International Consultation on English Texts. Enlarged and Revised Edition. Philadelphia: Fortress Press, 1972.

Charles P. Price for the Standing Liturgical Commission, *Introducing the Proposed Book. A Study of the Significance of the Proposed Book of Common Prayer for the Doctrine, Discipline, and Worship of the Episcopal Church* (Prayer Book Studies 29, Revised). New York: The Church Hymnal Corporation, 1976.

Francis Procter and Walter Howard Frere, *A New History of the Book of Common Prayer.* First Edition, 1855. Revised and Rewritten by Walter Howard Frere, 1901. Reprint. London: Macmillan & Co., 1955.

Massey Hamilton Shepherd, Jr., *The Oxford American Prayer Book Commentary.* New York: Oxford University Press, 1950.

Index